Tracey Moffatt Free-Falling

Tracey Moffatt
Free-Falling

Dia Center for the Arts, New York

Tracey Moffatt: Free-Falling
October 9, 1997–June 14, 1998
Dia Center for the Arts
548 West 22nd Street, New York City

Edited by Lynne Cooke and Karen Kelly

Designed by BUREAU, new york

Printed in Iceland by Oddi Ltd.

Library of Congress Catalog Card Number 98-84518

ISBN 0-944521-36-3

Distributed by
Distributed Art Publishers
155 6th Avenue, 2nd floor
New York, New York 10013
(800) 338-BOOK

Major funding for this exhibition was provided by the Lannan Foundation; The Andy Warhol Foundation for the Visual Arts; The Embassy of Australia, Washington, D.C.; and The Australia Council for the Arts; with an additional generous contribution by the Wolfensohn Family Foundation. This book was published with generous assistance from ArtPace, San Antonio; L. A. Galerie, Frankfurt; Matthew Marks Gallery, New York; Paul Morris Gallery, New York; and Roslyn Oxley9 Gallery, Paddington, Australia.

Tracey Moffatt: Free-Falling

7
Preface
Michael Govan

9
Only Angels Have Wings
Isaac Julien with Mark Nash

23
A Photo-Filmic Odyssey
Lynne Cooke

45
Dust
Sam Shepard

57
Biography, Bibliography, Checklist

Preface

Tracey Moffatt's exhibition "Free-Falling" is one of a series of ambitious projects by young artists that Dia has commissioned over the past decade in its galleries at 542 West 22nd Street. Both Moffatt's photographic series *Up in the Sky* and her video *Heaven* were made specifically for this presentation. Curator Lynne Cooke has augmented these new works with *Night Cries: A Rural Tragedy*, Moffatt's much-acclaimed early film, and *GUAPA (Good Looking)*, a photographic suite created in 1995 during Moffatt's residency at ArtPace in San Antonio.

The realization of "Free-Falling," Tracey Moffatt's first major museum show to date, and its corresponding publication are the result of the efforts of many individuals and institutions. In particular, we extend our warmest thanks to the artist, who approached this exhibition and the creation of these commissions with characteristic enthusiasm.

We are grateful for the insight of our sponsors in making the exhibition of this Australian artist possible; for their generous support, we would like to acknowledge the Lannan Foundation, the Andy Warhol Foundation for the Visual Arts, the Embassy of Australia, the Australia Council for the Arts, and the Wolfensohn Family Foundation. For the loan of *Night Cries: A Rural Tragedy*, we thank Women Make Movies.

In this book, Isaac Julien, a fellow filmmaker, along with his collaborator Mark Nash, and Dia's curator Lynne Cooke provide rich critical perspectives on Moffatt's work. Vintage Books gave us a unique opportunity to juxtapose Sam Shepard's evocative short story "Dust" with *Up in the Sky*. David Frankel and Phil Mariani lent their crucial editorial expertise. Bureau's dynamic design brings out the filmic nature of Moffatt's still imagery. This publication was realized with generous assistance from ArtPace, San Antonio; Matthew Marks Gallery, New York; Paul Morris Gallery, New York; L. A. Galerie, Frankfurt; and Roslyn Oxley9 Gallery, Paddington, Australia.

Michael Govan, *Director*

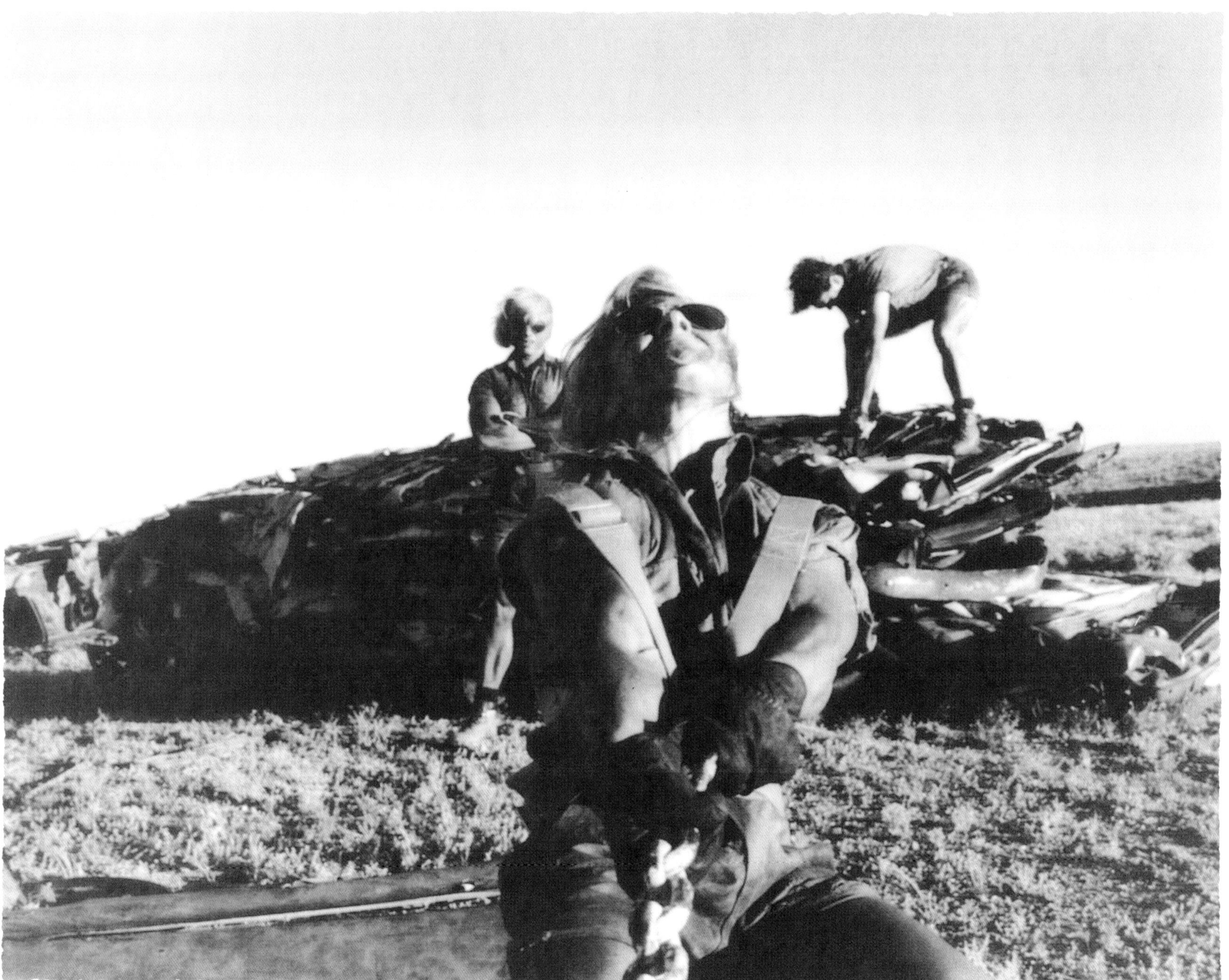

from *Up in the Sky*, 1997

Only Angels Have Wings

Isaac Julien with Mark Nash

April 21, 1987

Dear Sankofa Group,

My name is Tracey Moffatt. … I'm writing to introduce myself since I am coming to London shortly and would like to meet you all. I've known about your film group for a few years now. … I've been asked along with some other Aboriginal artists to attend an Arts Festival in Portsmouth in the South of England. Part of this festival will be a reenactment of the launching of the First Fleet, so it seems ridiculous that the organizers have asked us to attend this ceremony (the Queen will be present) when all it represents is the beginning of the invasion into our traditional lands. Therefore I am planning some sort of demonstration on the 13th of May in Portsmouth Harbour and I'm looking for support, especially from Black people. I have agreed to display my photographic work, this doesn't bother me, but I have no intention of standing around waving at a bunch of tall ships setting sail for Australia.

In April 1987 Sankofa (the black film and video collective that I cofounded in 1983), received this postcard from Tracey Moffatt. It would be only later that I would have the opportunity to see her black-and-white prints *Some Lads* (1986), showing urban Aboriginal youths from the Aboriginal and Islander Dance Company–mainly men in various poses of undress, playing and smiling, all very cute, some with dreadlocks, and with pumped chests à la Bruce Weber. These images introduced us to an urban Aboriginal artistic community that even looked like some of the members of our own film group. We felt an immediate identification with Tracey's work. In the same postcard, Tracey wrote that she had just finished a short film:

I'm also planning on bringing over my latest film called "Nice Colored Girls." It is a short (16 minutes) experimental piece which explores attitudes between white men and black women in this country [Australia] in an historical and contemporary context. Though the underlying purpose of the work is to illustrate the existence of a very real "urban Aboriginal culture."

We didn't get to see the film right away, but another postcard –to Martina Attille, another founding member of the collective, on June 21, 1987–pointed us toward it:

My film "Nice Colored Girls" was programmed with your film "Passion" [Passion of Remembrance, *1986] at the film festival. It was well received. ... I think audiences have found your film an interesting exercise, but I heard comments like "Oh, very BFI" [British Film Institute], which I wasn't sure of what was meant, comparisons with S [Sally] Potter's "Gold Diggers"!! ... I hate having to be the spy in the audience. ... My little film is currently on videotape sitting in Sheila Whittikar's office, London Film Festival, why don't you ring her and grab it and look at it. I'm very pleased with it.*

We couldn't wait—we were thrilled to be able to see it. *Nice Colored Girls* turned out to be a cheeky, irreverent short. A meditation on girls out on the town, hustling in the night, in Sydney's downtown Kings Cross area, this stylized experimental film gave us an insight into the lives of young "colored girls" searching for "capital." These young urban Aboriginal women are emblematic of the bad-gurrl protagonists of much of Tracey's work.

These women's nights out become a rather precarious occupation: for them to fully experience pleasure, a seduction of revenge has to take place. Showing us what desire looks like in this postcolonial exchange for money, *Nice Colored Girls* contrasts the relationship between these contemporary urban Aboriginal women and their "captains" (sugar daddies) with that between Aboriginal women and white-male colonists over two hundred years ago. Where Aboriginal women once went on board the colonists' ships and exchanged their bodies for bags of coin, their descendants seduce modern-day captains by getting them drunk, dancing with them, and eventually snatching their wallets. As the film's subtitles put it (mimicking the style of anthropological films), "We call them captains because our mothers and grandmothers have always called them that." These gurrls enjoy themselves now much as the colonists report they enjoyed themselves then. Now, of course, things have changed, but maybe not enough—these women still have to play with the colonial masters to earn a living.

Moffatt's cinema has always involved dislocations of time and space, apparent in *Nice Colored Girls* through cuts between the Aboriginal girls' nightly rituals of seduction and a series of historical reenactments. In a film studio, an etching hanging on a wall in an ornate gilt frame shows a coastline with a European ship moored in the distance. In the foreground, with their backs to us, Aboriginal figures stand looking out over the bay. The camera backtracks, we hear contemporary street sounds, a rope ladder abruptly falls in front of the wall where the picture hangs, and all of a sudden several Aboriginal women climb up it as we hear a voice-over from a journal of an early English male settler. His narration of an interracial encounter is permeated with colonialist desire for the Other.

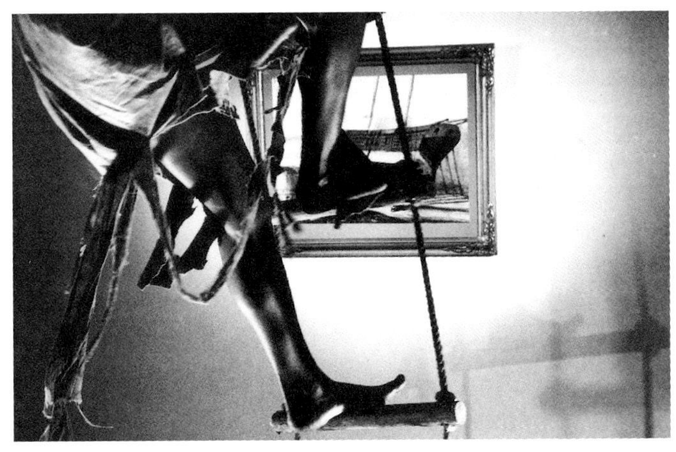

still from *Nice Colored Girls*, 1987

This play with the picture and frame recalls Jean-Luc Godard and Jean-Pierre Gorin's *Tout va bien* of 1972, and, in fact, *Nice Colored Girls* is imbued with antirealist film strategies. In its attempt to avoid a linear narrative style, the film is reacting against the realist tradition of documentary or ethnographic film. It also comments on that tradition in its use of subtitling and in its foregrounding of artifice, decor, and color; throughout, it avoids the clichés of realist enactment. *Nice Colored Girls* immediately gave us an impression of Tracey as an artist interested in a Brechtian kind of critical distance as an act of political subversion, representing girls who have to behave badly through economic necessity but who refuse to be made to feel guilty because of that. Maybe Tracey was a bad gurrl herself. Indeed we were not disappointed when we met her.

I met Tracey again in 1991 when Mark Nash and I went to Australia to show my film *Young Soul Rebels* at the Sydney Film Festival shortly after its screening in Cannes. Tracey was working on the script for a film of her own, *Bedevil*, which eventually screened during the director's fortnight in Cannes in 1993. Tracey struck me as a charming postmodern artist. During our visit, I sensed that she felt quite alone in Australia, but she treasured her isolation in a way: it forced her to concentrate. She couldn't spend time being vocal about people's indifference to her concerns and just had to get on with making work, which was indeed what she did. She spoke of how much the Australian audience had liked my *Looking for Langston* (1989), and said she had been impressed not only by its visuality but also by its beautiful actors (boys being an interest we both shared). In my mind's eye, I had already identified Tracey as one of the mixed-race angels in my film who peer down from the balcony, their eyes beams of light that shine on human subjects who have been shunned and excluded. In a way, she was like Walter Benjamin's angel of history:

His face is turned toward the past. Where we perceive a chain of events, he sees one single catastrophe which keeps piling wreckage upon wreckage and hurls it in front of his feet. The angel would like to stay, awaken the dead, and make whole what has been smashed. But a storm is blowing from Paradise; it has got caught in his wings with such violence that the angel can no longer close them. This storm irresistibly propels him into the future to which his back is turned, while the pile of debris before him grows skyward.[1]

1 Walter Benjamin, "Theses on the Philosophy of History," in *Illuminations*, ed. Hannah Arendt, trans. Harry Zohn (1968; reprint New York: Schocken Books, 1978), pp. 257–58.

In Sankofa, Martina Attille and I recognized Tracey as a kindred spirit, working with similar themes but on the other side of the world—part of a diasporic exchange, part of her "network of like-minded artists." More important, we shared her aesthetic interest in artifice, style, and the tableau. Martina's short film *Dreaming Rivers* (1988) also shared Tracey-like aesthetics, and was shown along with *Nice Colored Girls* on England's Channel 4 TV in 1991. Form, light, color, mise-en-scène were foregrounded in Tracey's films and photographs, cutting across the restrictions of realist documentary, a category of visual production rooted in ethnography that we almost instinctively distrusted—not just because it usually misrepresented the lives of working-class or black people, but also because the strategies used by traditional documentaries to explore questions of racial difference and discrimination were too questionably informational, and simply "fixing."

When Lynne Cooke of the Dia Center for the Arts asked me to write an essay for this catalogue, she said that she wasn't asking me as a black artist but as someone who knew something of Tracey and admired her work, and who, through my own work, was familiar not only with film but with the placement of both film and installation in the art world. When I spoke to Tracey about the essay, she replied, "If you write about me as a woman artist of color I will kill you!" This extremely humorous joke was a response, I think, to the fact that critics writing about Tracey's work tend to emphasize her ethnicity and often ignore the extent to which her work explores constructions of whiteness and masculinity in postcolonial Australia, and the interdependency of Aboriginal cultures with the so-called white Australian culture. As someone whose work contests positionings like "artist of color," I would be last to reinstitute them. Still, even if Tracey's art is in no way defined by race and gender difference, it is clearly and crucially inflected by her particular experience of their effects, which contribute to it some of its most potent themes.

Tracey's art looks back to the psychic terrors and desires of the colonial past to make sense of the future. Other Australia-based women artists deal with some of these concerns (Laleen Jayamanne, for example, in her *Song of Ceylon* of 1985), but I haven't seen any doing so in such an accomplished way, free of the dictates of theoretical fashion. (It is often forgotten that Australia was at the vanguard of postmodern theory—publishing the translations in English of Michel Foucault, for example.) Dia's "Free-Falling" show is Tracey's first large-scale exhibition in New York. Presenting provocative work in film, photography, and video installation, it establishes her as an artist of international stature. The elements of the exhibition present different, often opposed, aesthetic strategies, but by looking more closely, we can tease out some of the continuities.

Bad Gurrls/Badd Blaks

The video installation *Heaven* (1997) appropriates the fetishistic gaze usually attributed to the masculine imaginary and turns it back on men. White and black surfers at Sydney's Bondi Beach habitually change in and out of their swimming trunks on the street; Tracey finds them cloaking themselves in towels, or sheltering behind their cars. Interrupting this circuit in which men are usually seen only by one another, Tracey treats it as a performance staged for her camera. Of course, she chooses only the most beautiful boys to photograph. Later, however, she undercuts their narcissism by daring them to expose themselves to her. Some are cocksure, some regress into heterosexual mooning, others turn coy, struggling with their briefs in the confines of their cars. Ten years after *Nice Colored Girls*, we find one of the bad-gurrl characters now let loose on Bondi Beach, accosting surfers rather than captains, giving up watching for wallets in Kings Cross and taking up the camera to cruise for butts in Bondi.

Despite *Heaven*'s elements of erotic tease, it actually draws attention to the distinction between penis and phallus. The sculpted bodies of the surfers may be phallically masterful, but we see them at the limp-penis stage—not at their moment of physical glory, the moment of surfing, but skulking in their cars before or after it. These carefully modeled bodies end up becoming signs of the vulnerability and naïveté of masculinity. The soundtrack, similarly, has nothing to do with the action on the street. Although we see the men speaking, we do not hear their voices; instead we hear the crash of waves, interwoven with Tibetan drumming. The image of masculinity, then, is stripped of the *sound* of masculinity; the men are thus reduced to their images. Yet the sounds of both drums and sea—where Tracey, had she chosen to, could have photographed the surfers in glorious physical display—connote realms of masculinity. The fetishistic gaze, then, is displaced from the imaged body into a world it cannot actually see, the world implied by the sound of the sea and the drums. In all these respects, *Heaven* is a particularly irreverent example of a common effort in feminist and avant-garde cinema: an attempt to debunk some of the more oppressive tropes of heterosexuality.

Heaven is shown on a TV monitor, the small scale of the image reinforcing the video's intimacy. *Night Cries: A Rural Tragedy* (1989), though a short film, is a full-scale movie in its style and effect. It tells the story of a middle-aged Aboriginal woman forced to care for the ancient invalid white woman by whom she was adopted as a child. The characters are based on those of the 1955 Australian classic *Jedda* (directed by Charles Chauvel), one of the earliest Australian films to address the predicament of Aboriginal people being incorporated into a racist society. In *Night Cries*, the characters are presented as if thirty years older than in *Jedda* and living out their days alone in a now very decayed and cobwebbed studio-set homestead in the middle of a painted-backdrop desert.

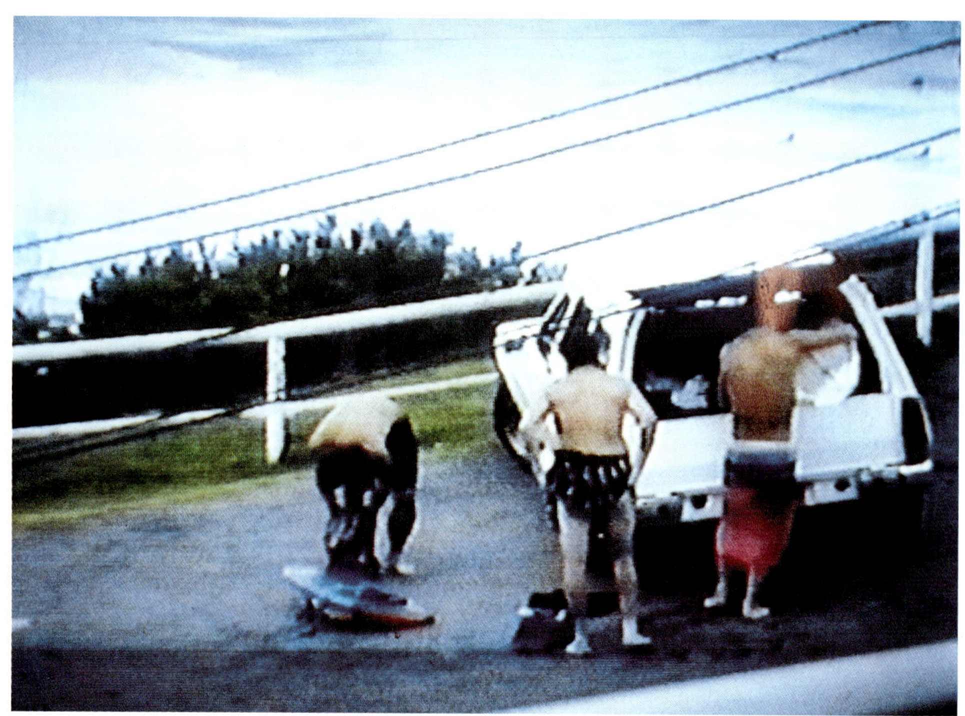

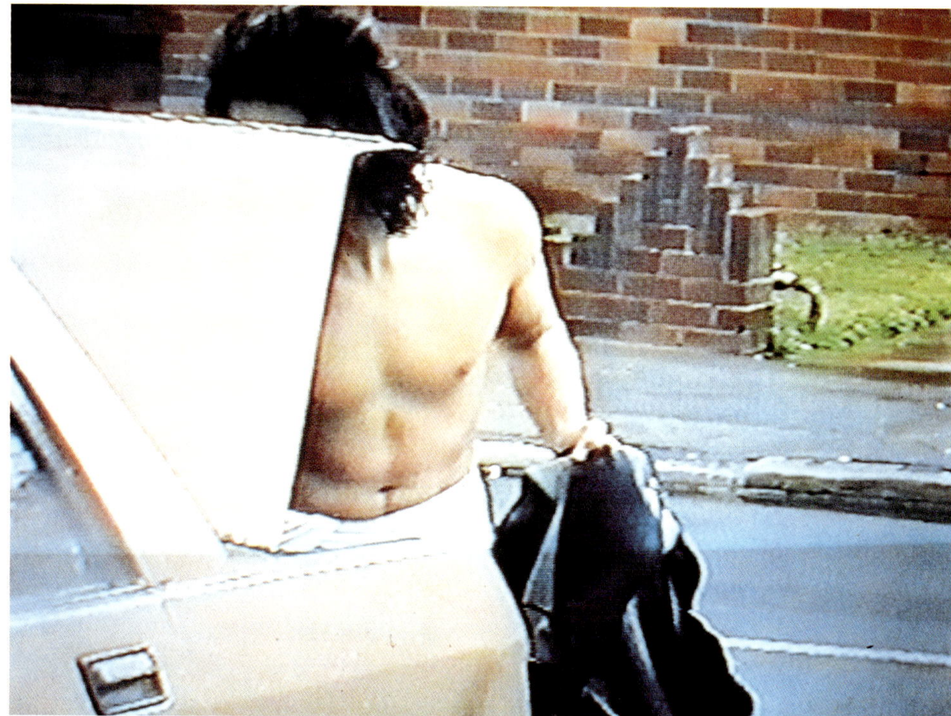

stills from *Heaven*, 1997

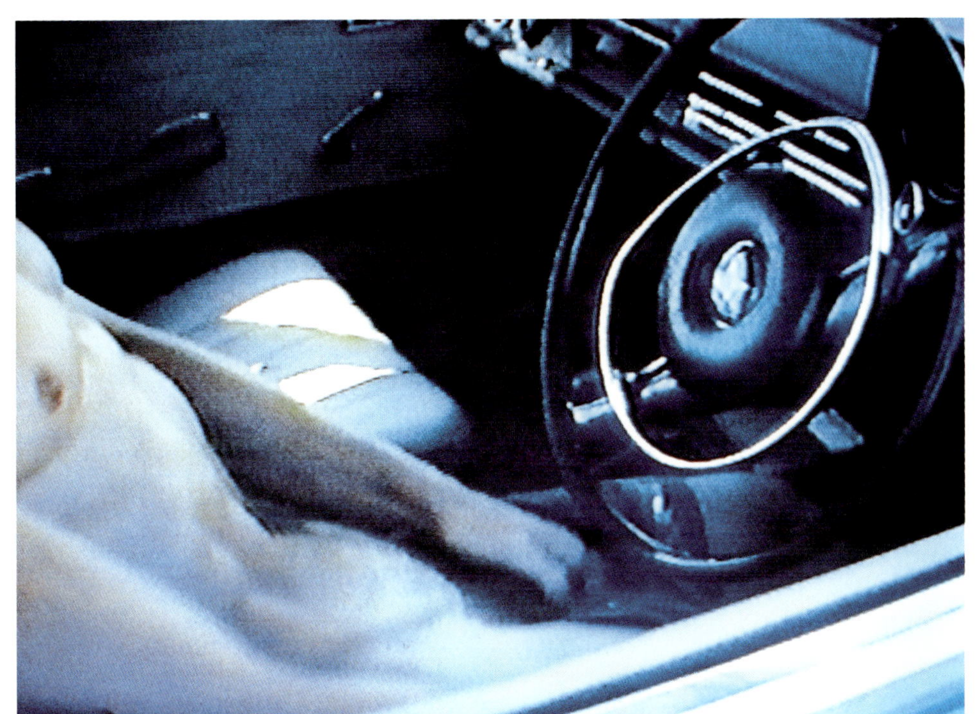

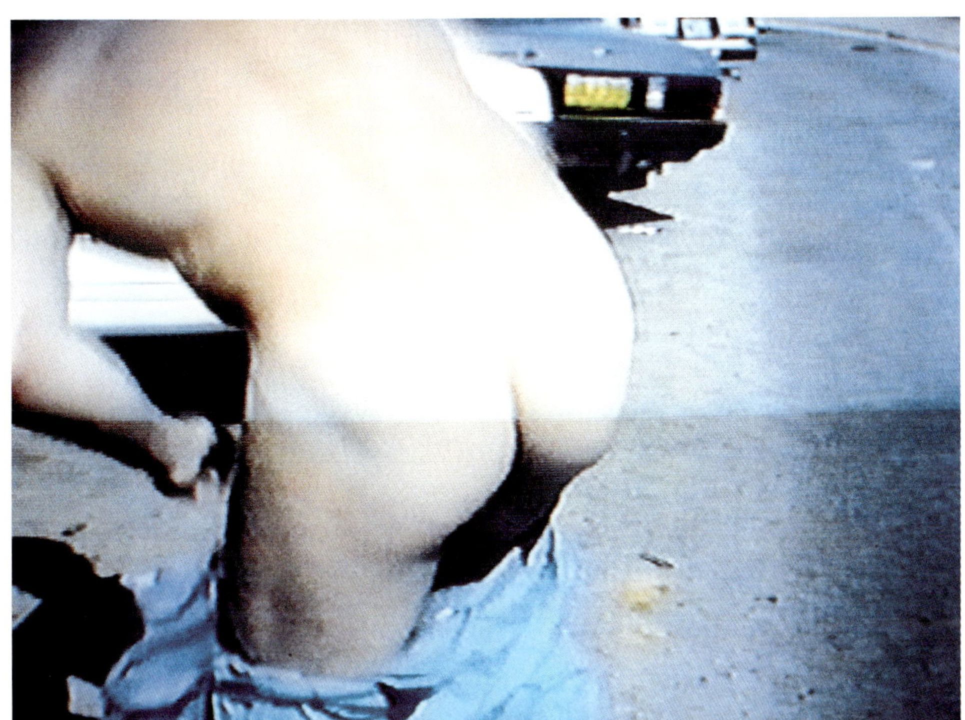

Documentary films like Alec Morgan's *Lousy Little Sixpence* (1984) have also exposed the assimilationist policies of successive Australian governments that aimed to erase Aboriginal culture, for instance, the so-called Aboriginal Protection Board's forced removal of Aboriginal children into white foster homes to be used as slave labor between 1909 and 1930 (just as the early colonists had attempted to remove Aboriginal people altogether). *Night Cries* takes a more emotionally complex and ambiguous tack, dealing with the intricate scenarios of love and dependency that develop in mother-daughter relationships, whether biological or "cultural" (in, say, cases of adoption).

The two women in *Night Cries* participate in a "rural tragedy" of colonial domesticity. The film is shot through by diegetic cuts describing a stylized Salvador Dali–type landscape, the frame for the perverse relationships of domesticity, which are seen through a series of tableaux vivants featuring an old white "mother" who is brutishly but not unaffectionately served by a darker-skinned "daughter." The rendering of this "moment of hybridity"[2] is heightened by the colorful artifice of Tracey's painterly eye, as elements of narrative, biographical, or ethnographic interest are eclipsed in favor of phantasmatic scenarios. The mother-daughter relationship is a recurring motif across all of Tracey's work.

Terra Nullius

Only in the last decade have Aboriginal peoples been able to establish legal recognition for themselves in the Australian state. The original genocidal campaigns of colonialism, along with subsequent expropriations and forced removals, were based on a sophistry developed by the British, who described Australia as an empty, uninhabited country (terra nullius). The colonists decided, in other words, that the continent they had "discovered" was empty of human life. Since Aboriginal peoples were not really human, they could simply be treated as animals, and exterminated. No need for treaties or agreements; the Europeans could just move in. Missionaries were sent out into this arid desert of a continent to try and convert its "savages" not just to Christianity but, in the process, to "humanity." Aboriginal children and the inevitably increasing population of mixed-race children were removed to orphanages and foster homes (the official policy of "due care"), eventually growing up to provide a source of cheap domestic and industrial labor. After a long legal battle waged by Aboriginal groups, the ideology behind this policy was finally overturned by the Australian High Court's *Mabo* decision in June 1992 (which established a concept of "native title" to land) that would take precedence over that imposed by the colonists. The present Australian government is seeking, without the agreement of Aboriginal people, to override the 1993 Native Title Act, which was passed as the result of negotiations with Aboriginal and non-Aboriginal interests and the government following *Mabo*. If successful, it will remove native title rights over large tracts of land.

2 I quote Homi Bhabha's term for the condition of the mixed-race postcolonial subject, for whom a simple racial identity is not possible, but who finds inventive and creative modes of living racially or indeed sexually diverse identities.

The adoption policy is one of the primal scenes for Tracey's work, evidenced both in *Night Cries* and in the ghostly *Up in the Sky* (1997), a series of offset prints presenting staged images masquerading as documentary ones. One photograph, taken from inside a shabby shack, allows a glimpse of three nuns outside, framed in the window like sinister crows waiting to seize their prey–a brown baby in the arms of a white woman. In another photo, a trio of nuns toss the baby between them. Elsewhere two children play in the shadow of an embankment, which has the hieratic stillness of an Egyptian pyramid. One wears a nurse's uniform, the other stands blindfolded. In another photograph, the carcass of a dead cow hangs in a tree shot through by the sun's rays, while two butch-looking women, apparently about to be interrupted by a third protagonist, argue below.

These are scenes of lives in what appear to be squatter camps. Black and white figures wrestle in the dust; car-wreckers stand astride smashed vehicles; a crowd of black and white villagers line the street, witnessing something of the commotion introduced by the intrusive camera. The scenes evoke images of Outback life familiar from beer and car commercials on TV, as well as from documentaries exposing the abjectness to which both Aboriginal and poor white ("white trash") communities have been condemned. At the same time, the figuring of the white protagonists suggests other scenes: Tracey seems to have been influenced by Pasolini's imaging of the slums outside Rome. Neither *Accattone* nor George Mitchell's Mad Max films, *Up in the Sky* could nevertheless almost be a recently discovered set of production stills from such films. These images were shot in the abandoned mining area of Broken Hill in southeastern Australia, where many commercials as well as the Mad Max series were shot–a "junky Australian landscape" where Moffatt found people ready to pose for her.[3] Everyone desires the Warholian moment.

The mesmerizing stare on the face of a white girl is frozen, abandoned. As she sits in a metal tub, waiting for "something more," a rough, tattooed young white man walks along, smiling to himself. White townsfolk return our gaze as they look out of the picture frame, as if waiting for the director to say "Action!" before a crowd scene begins. Dazed by a car's headlights, a crazed white man crawls across the road–the cliché of Aboriginal abjection in the white imaginary. Then he crawls back. In this science-fiction Australia, some roles are reversed, bringing the elements of fantasy in our imagining of them closer to home. We also find a counter-reading to terra nullius–in a sense, it is now the white race that is abandoned. Tracey focuses her affinity with and ambivalence toward these landscapes through her staged reenactments, which look as if they might come from film, television, or *Life* magazine spreads from the fifties. A reworking of the master narrative of race relations is a recurring motif; the scenes are thoroughly implanted with demonstrations of interracial interdependence, and also of a gendered subjectivity.

3 Sonya Voumard, "The Moffatt Mosaic," *The Australian Way* (Qantas inflight magazine), (August 1996).

Ars Nullius–Video, Film, Photography

Whereas a number of contemporary artists (Cindy Sherman, Robert Longo, Rebecca Horn, Julian Schnabel)[4] have been fascinated by mainstream cinema, Tracey is one of several artists making the opposite move from film and video to the gallery, presenting moving and still images together in the space of art. Avant-garde and experimental film has moved closer to the art world in recent years, separating itself from more mainstream narrative cinema, which may have incorporated some of its innovations but has rejected its radical vision. Hollywood and the art world are opposed on the question of meaning: where Hollywood likes meaning to be self-evident (but often makes it either inconsequential or a reinforcement of conventional systems of understanding), postmodern art of the nineties is concerned with meaning's absence, or with the suspension of narrative. There is, to adapt Frank Kermode's phrase, no longer any sense in having an ending at all. Tracey's work is emblematic here: abandoned somewhere in Australia (somewhere reminiscent of one of the settlements clustered along the trans-Australian railroad, and occasionally visited by documentary filmmakers and social workers), we are at some kind of crossroads. In terms of race, the assimilationist narrative has been eviscerated; but there is no utopian multicultural narrative to take its place.

The narrative of progress has been replaced by a series of Manichean encounters, such as the staged roller-derby encounters in the photo series *GUAPA (Good Looking)* (1995).[5] The black and white female contestants enact violent encounters with one another and with the (white) male referee. Is this the fantasy assimilationist arena of American sports (the series was made during a residency in Texas)? Or a semisublimated enactment of racial and sexual antagonisms? The photographs are tinted in soft rose-sepia pastel shades that could evoke advertisements for feminine products, further confusing the viewer as to what is really at stake. As distilled, hyperstylized simulations of photojournalism in old *Life* magazines from the fifties, they contest an already established documentary format. These women are formidable-looking people and are clearly having fun.

Here and elsewhere, Tracey deploys a kind of absence of signification, achieved not by draining the signifier of its significance but by deriving it from precontextualized elements that are nevertheless cut off from subjective and autobiographical narratives. The images, then, are floating, as if in a time capsule, left for some future civilization to determine their meaning, which is almost on the verge of being lost. When I was teaching cinema studies at New York University recently, I was able to see Tracey's film *Moodeitj-Yorgas (Solid Women)* (1988), a series of documentary video interviews with Aboriginal women in Western Australia, interrupted by visual and auditory dislocations. Confirming that Tracey's insight into Australian national identity and artistic cultural practices could only be

4 See Mike O'Pray, "Movie Wannabes," *Art Monthly*, no. 210 (October 1997), pp. 1–6.

5 Televised with great popularity in the seventies, roller derby contests—with their snarling, bumptious skaters engaged in what appeared to be mortal combat—exemplify Tracey's identification of sport as the synthesis of theater and violence. To emulate roller derby's tough female competitors, Tracey hired models with thick muscular bodies, and clothed them in costumes produced by a local Texan seamstress. See Tracey Moffatt, "Diary of a Texas Art Residency," in *Tracey Moffatt: Fever Pitch* (Annandale, Australia: Piper Press, 1995), pp. 5–12.

postcolonial and postmodern, *Moodeitj-Yorgas* problematizes the conventional first-person interview strategy with out-of-sync sound. Meanwhile, her questioning of Aboriginality, and her view of it and whiteness as interrelated, undermine the binaristic positioning of Europeans and Otherness so prevalent in race relations. *Moodeitj-Yorgas* began a process of healing the ontological and narcissistic wounds of nonwhite subjects; while Tracey's inventory of hybrid representations moved toward the possibility of a métisse or creole society, it also acknowledged the value and ethics of Aboriginal cultures. And the film's status as a series of experimental video portraits emphasized its own technological and electronic form, announcing the death of realistic ethnographic documentary practice and the birth of a more aesthetic, self-reflexive art.

The question of resignification is crucial to Tracey. Contesting the cheap race-relations sociology that would condemn the nonwhite artist to performing the Other, she refuses any fixity that would correspond to the categories of identity politics. What could it mean, in fact, for an artist to be fixated on codes of racial difference while not prioritizing the question of visual form? Tracey is one of a number of "bad gurrl/badd blak" women artists–Kara Walker comes to mind as another–who seek to avoid the burden of black representation by hyperbolic use of stereotypes. Race signifies and creates meaning in our readings of visual representations, but Tracey's work is also about the impossibility of a calculus of the multiple tragedies of race and colonialism–the "modern tragedy" according to Raymond Williams in his book of the same name, which is distinguished by the impossibility of extrapolating from the Greek and Shakespearean tragedy of the individual to the tragedy of a whole social group.[6] Haunted by a colonial past, we can use Tracey's work to reposition ourselves through what she brings of modernity to this landscape. Whiteness and Otherness are transformed in this encounter.

Lacanian analyst Danuza Machado has compared the relations, on the one hand, between analysis and the analysand, and on the other, between the work of art and the viewer. She says,

The work of art is something that doesn't make sense, it proliferates sense. … It is something that provokes in the viewer a turning point like the psychoanalytic act. … [Like] any form of entertainment, it is a way out of the malaise of daily life, it makes you think about your situation.[7]

It is this daily malaise of race relations that Tracey wants to shake up. In *Up in the Sky*, there is a photograph of a dark-skinned Aboriginal man staring up into the sky. Behind him, a sunset glows across a mountain. In another image, an Aboriginal baby lies on a bed behind a broken wall. Which is the past? Which is

6
See Raymond Williams, *The Modern Tragedy* (London: Verso Editions, 1979).

7
Danuza Machado, "A Little Object," interview by Alex Potts, *AN* (previously *Artists Newsletter*) (September 1997), pp. 10–13.

the future? Moffatt provides various pairings and triplings in her displays of images in "Free-Falling," inviting the viewer to imagine these images like film stills–stills, however, that do not let the viewer imagine a single narrative but offer differing, contested ones. The possibility of uniting these disparate fragments (and their implied profilmic reality) is promised in the aesthetics of the display, but then withheld. *Up in the Sky* evokes the ontological and narcissistic injuries that are performed on the body of the Other.

As Françoise Vergès has written in a discussion of anamnesis, the work of thought, "A group can express what is still lacking or still to come only through a redistribution of its past. From the knowledge of the past, of the conditions that made it such, a group can decide what is lacking, for instance freedom or equality."[8] Moffatt's work is about exposing or exploring some of those gaps in representation. It both evokes the injuries of the colonial past and imagines other scenarios, such as those of *Up in the Sky*, which thus can be imagined differently, even transcended. A phantasmatic repetition of the loss and injury that Aboriginal peoples, among others, have suffered, her art is about reparation. It is about the possibilities of working through those experiences to move beyond issues of identity. Opening the grave, freeing the ghosts whose presence haunts the living, is not only essential to understanding, it is also an essential part of her art.

8 Françoise Vergès, "Chains of Madness, Chains of Colonialism," in *The Fact of Blackness*, ed. Alan Reid (London: ICA, 1996), p.64.

We are grateful to David Frankel for his editorial scholarship; to Martina Attille for access to her Tracey Moffatt archive; to Coco Fusco for advice and comments; to Glen Masato Mimura for his paper "Black Memories, Tracey Moffatt's *Bedevil*," which he presented at the conference "Featuring Paradise: Representations of the Pacific in Film," at the University of Hawaii at Manoa in November 1997; to Karen Kelly and Lynne Cooke; and to Tracey Moffatt herself.

Isaac Julien
is an artist and filmmaker who is currently a visiting lecturer in Afro-American studies and visual and environmental studies at Harvard University. His most recent film is *Frantz Fanon: Black Skin White Mask* (1996), most recently screened at the 38th Film Festival Dei Popoli, Italy, and his most recent installations are *Trussed* at the Walter Phillips Gallery in Banff and *Fanon S.A.*, shown at the 2nd Johannesburg Biennal 1997.

Mark Nash
is a lecturer in film history and theory at the University of East London and produced and cowrote *Frantz Fanon*.

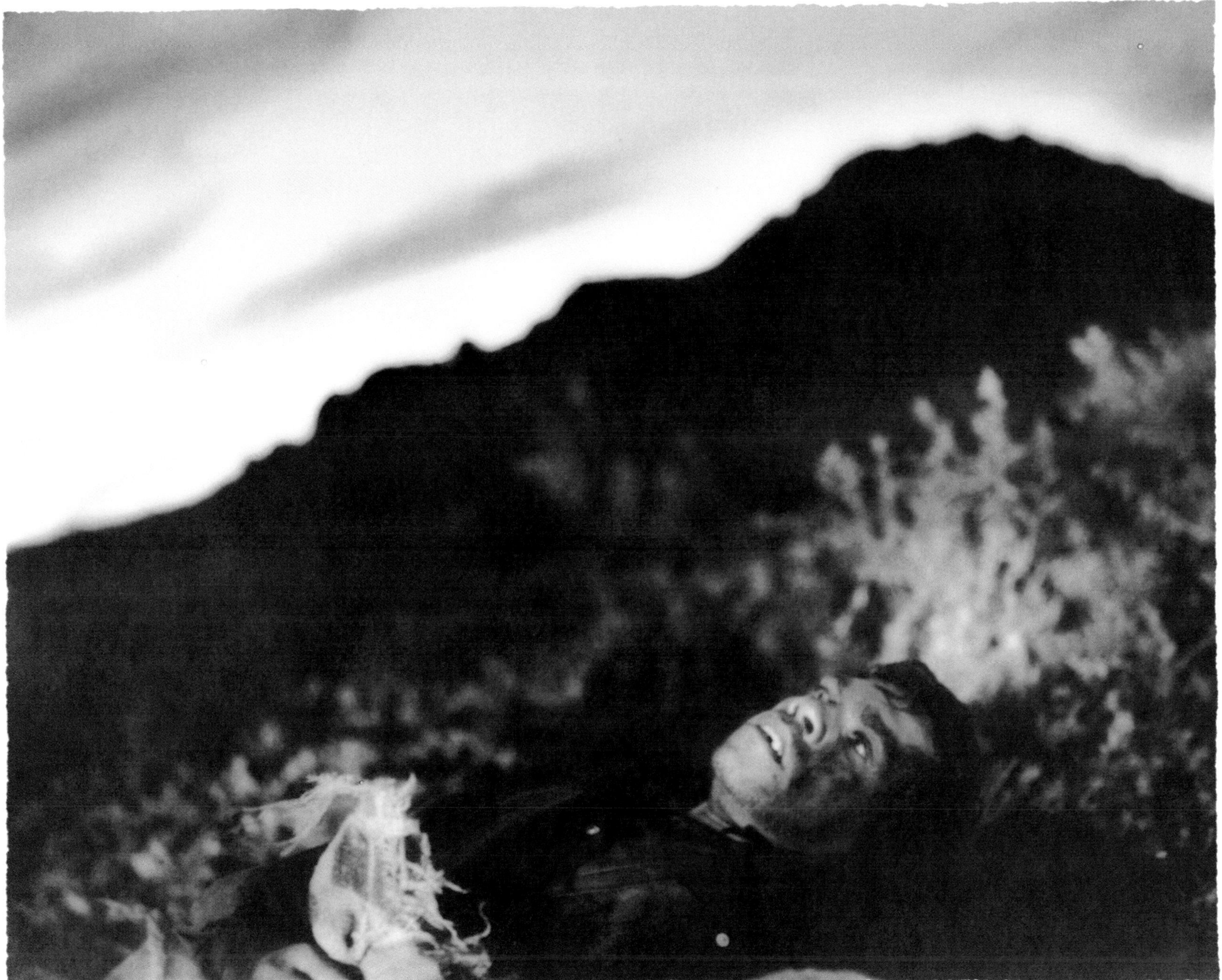

from *Up in the Sky*, 1997

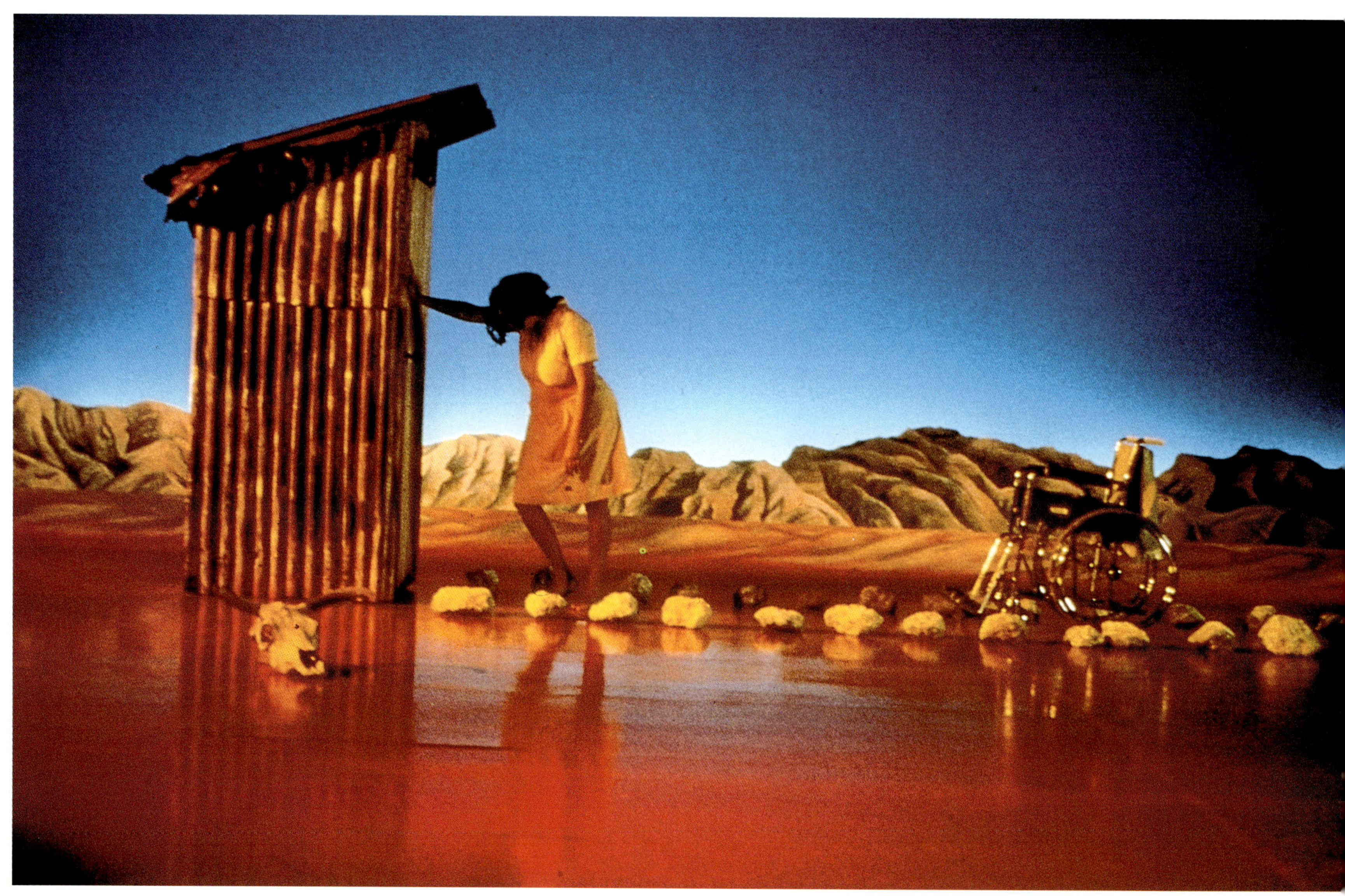

still from *Night Cries: A Rural Tragedy*, 1989

A Photo-Filmic Odyssey

Lynne Cooke

I am not concerned with versimilitude ... I am not concerned with capturing reality, I'm concerned with creating it myself.

—— Tracey Moffatt

I am not recognized as an inventor of stylistic formulae, but for the degree of intensity to which I bring the contamination and mixture of styles.

—— Pier Paolo Pasolini

Tracey Moffatt was catapulted to critical attention on the cusp of the 1990s on the basis of two quite distinct works made almost simultaneously: a nine-part phototableau, titled *Something More*, and a 35 mm short film, *Night Cries: A Rural Tragedy* (both made in 1989). Increasingly overlaying, intersecting, even interrogating each other, these two media remain the cornerstone of her practice as a visual artist, notwithstanding occasional forays into video and music television.[1]

Something More is comprised of both color and black-and-white photographs, each 39⅜ by 51⅛ inches, organized along a three-tiered grid. The intermittent placement of the trio of monochromatic works serendipitously interrupts the smooth flow of the "storyboarded" narrative. The resulting discontinuity, a kind of Brechtian device that stimulates a reflexivity in the viewer, impairs the seductive unfolding of what is a familiar, even clichéd, fable of shattered aspirations and failed dreams. A young woman, born in the margins with few options, embraces stereotypical delusions of the romance, riches, and glamour of urban life. Redolent of sagas like Tennessee Williams's *Baby Doll* and Erskine Caldwell's *Tobacco Road*, with the Deep South finding its counterpart here in the Outback, *Something More* is at once local and generic. The telltale red earth and brilliant searing light, hallmarks of the Australian desert, are presented unmistakeably as broadly painted flats. They provide a backdrop for the opening photograph, which depicts a scene played out as if on a stage, with all the principals present. This is also the sole occasion on which the face of the central protagonist is revealed. Thereafter, aspirations and desire are manifest via detail; key attributes—notably, dress (and undress) and

1
Focusing on Moffatt's work as a visual artist, this essay includes a discussion of *Night Cries* since it alone among her films has been exhibited in gallery spaces, both as video projection and on a single monitor.

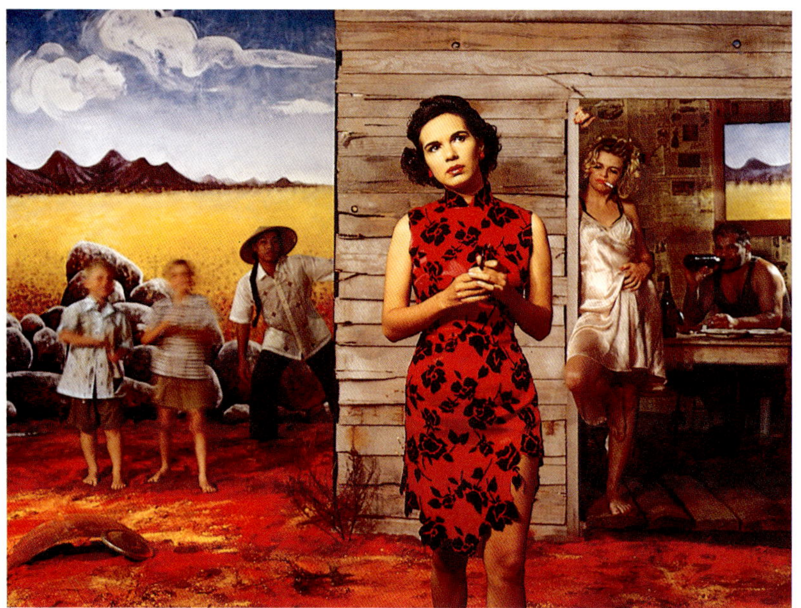

from *Something More*, 1989

weaponry—serve as surrogate agents in images that owe more to film than theater: the blurred motion, close-ups, low camera angles, and oblique sight lines all derive from cinematography.

Moffatt is able to render her version of this narrative, given its established precedents in both film and literature, in telegrammatically brief episodes, an approach reinforced by the manner in which, structurally as well as compositionally, *Something More* cleaves to conventions filmic rather than photographic. With the exception of the final image, individual frames appear to have been extracted from a larger sequence. By contrast, the concluding photograph, in resembling a movie still, adheres to a different genre and, consequently, does not so much freeze a moment as condense an entire drama.[2]

Certain features in Moffatt's rendition of this well-rehearsed tale are critical for her future work. The conflict—a rivalry between women—not only reverses conventional roles but invites a reading in racial terms. The bottle-blonde, who has become the antagonist, also inhabits the land to which her mixed-race counterpart (played by Moffatt) has only a dispropriated relation. The site of the drama is rural, far from the big city (Brisbane) yet dialectically connected to it. Sex and violence are closely intertwined, with, tellingly, the female aggressor assuming macho signifiers while the males are reduced to minor parts, as indifferent or ineffectual bystanders. Retelling this hackneyed fable through a local dialect, Moffatt deftly uses paraphrase and pastiche, not to imbue it with a compelling sense of singularity and specificity, novelty and poignancy, but by insisting wryly on its ubiquity and normality—locating the archetype within the stereotype, the mythic within the mass cultural.

In many respects, *Night Cries* could be deemed the reverse of *Something More*, even though again artifice and stylization inform Moffatt's visual language, and again a fundamental and paradigmatic relationship constitutes her point of departure, the mother-daughter bond. Manifestly contrived, its mise-en-scène owes as much to theater and painting as to film, while the storyline is structured into a continuous narrative in the present with two flashbacks to the daughter's childhood. The dramaturgical presentation of contemporary events in the homestead contrasts

2 Although on occasion individual frames have subsequently been exhibited singly, they gain their meaning and, arguably, their force, only within the context of the whole.

with the cinematic character of the flashbacks, evoking childhood nightmares of abandonment, and with the Caravaggesque depiction of the foot-washing scene, which generates a cherished memory of a reciprocated tending. The languorous unfolding of *Night Cries* leaves individual frames often suspended in time, so that they come to resemble phototableaux. Conjuring allusions to the most esteemed Australian art—the landscape paintings of Arthur Boyd and his peers—Moffatt's backdrop is also subversively infused with afterimages from the contemporaneous watercolors of Albert Namatjira: though the first Aboriginal artist working in a Western idiom to have attracted widespread popular acclaim, Namatjira has never been sanctioned by the academy for whom his antimodernist, formulaic manner is retrograde, facile, even kitschy. In short, naturalism is eschewed at every register, and formally, structurally, and thematically, impurities, simulations, and surrogates constantly infiltrate *Night Cries*, invalidating or contaminating the authentic, the established, the canonical, and the normative.

Moffatt's experience accords with this story, told as it is from the younger woman's perspective and across racial boundaries. Longing and loss, need and dependency are vividly evoked in abbreviated yet eloquent terms as devotion and duty contest with a desire for separation and self-determination. In the final scene in which the bereft Aboriginal daughter assumes a fetal position on a railway siding next to her dead, white foster mother, the setting is significantly a place of transition, a site of departure, suggesting that she is reenacting her recurrent nightmare of abandonment in infancy and, simultaneously, confronting the possibility of rebirth, of a new life.

While strategically drawing on song, Moffatt dispenses with dialogue in her deft and probing exploration of the maternal bond. Cut into and framing the narrative are extracts of celebrated country singer Jimmy Little crooning "Royal Telephone," the ballad that established his career and fame. Among the earliest Aboriginal entertainers to win national acclaim, Little's success in the late fifties was predicated on a polished assimilation of mainstream modes. His rise to stardom coincides chronologically with the point of departure of *Night Cries*, that is, with the childhood of Jedda, the heroine of Charles Chauvel's 1956 feature of that name, and the model for Moffatt's filmic daughter.

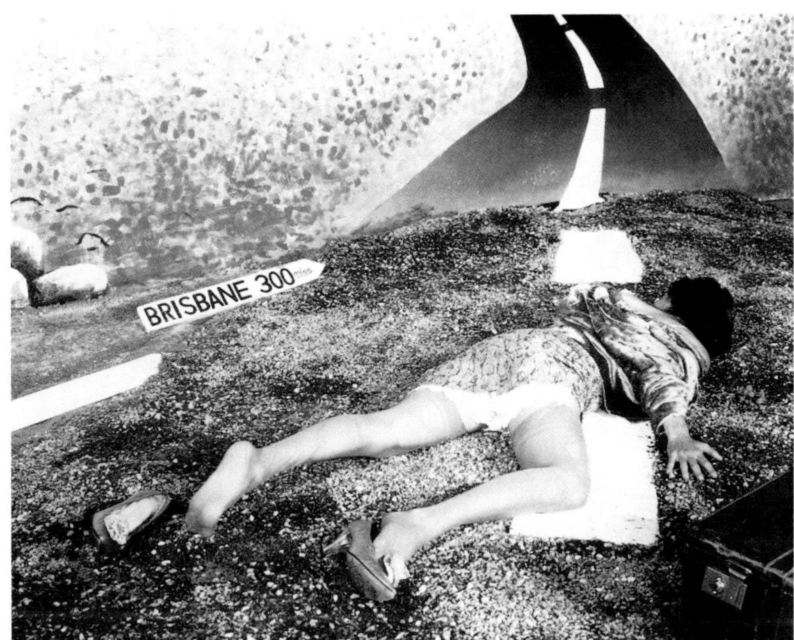

from *Something More*, 1989

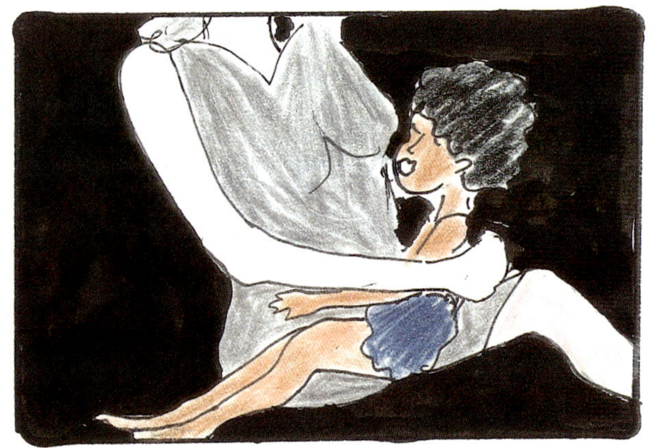

from storyboard for *Night Cries: A Rural Tragedy*, 1989

Regarded as a pioneering classic of Australian cinema, Chauvel's film explored the dilemma faced by Aboriginal people entering a racist society. *Jedda* examines their predicament through the figure of an Aboriginal orphan brought up by a station owner's wife, who, dissenting from her husband, believes that white society can offer Jedda broader options than those provided by her native culture, but only if the child is zealously shielded from tribal traditions and values. The adult Jedda experiences competing cultural claims, manifest as a rivalry between two suitors (one Aborigine assimilated, the other not), in ways that inevitably lead to her destruction. In relation to Chauvel, whose narrative pivots ambiguously on the question of whether biological destiny not only overwhelms but outweighs the impact of cultural conditioning, Moffatt explores a counter position, one rooted in a postcolonial situation. In her rewriting, Jedda's destiny is no longer determined by an erotically based relationship but resides in one that is even more fundamental, the maternal bond.

Moffatt's reorienting and updating of Chauvel's narrative not only makes women the sole protagonists in *Night Cries*, but revises gender representations. Empowering her Jedda with male-identified skills, specifically those of a stockman (implied in a scene in which she dexterously wields a stock whip), she suggests that the contemporary female has a potential for self-sufficiency and self-determination very different from that of her predecessor, whose fate was always to be dependent: either within a traditional native milieu or as wife to the station manager. The film also involves a rethinking of the tenets of assimilation by means of the figure of Little, who is shown miming himself, lip-syncing his hit song. Colonial mimicry, as Homi Bhabha argues, is based in the desire for a reformed, recognizable Other, a subject marked by a difference that is "almost the same, but not quite." Mimicry is thus the sign of a double articulation, "a complex strategy of reform, regulation, and discipline, which 'appropriates' the Other as it visualizes power ... [and] also the sign of the inappropriate, ... [of] a difference or recalcitrance, which

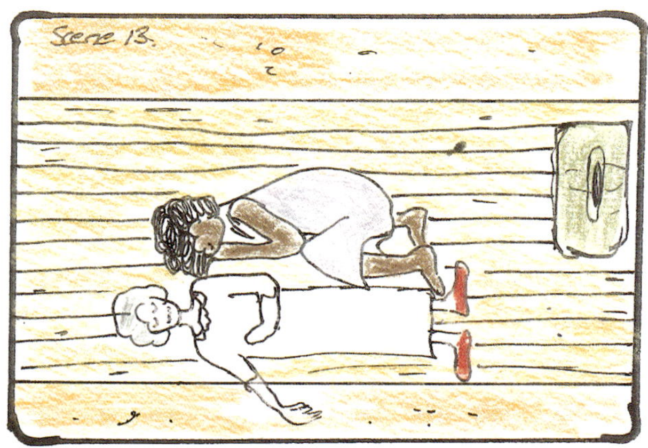

from storyboard for *Night Cries: A Rural Tragedy*, 1989

coheres the dominant strategic function of colonial power, intensifies surveillance, and poses an immanent threat to both 'normalized' knowledges and disciplinary powers."[3] Insidiously ironic, the manifestly slick performance Little gives for *Night Cries* suggests that his relationship to mainstream culture is–as are all relationships based in assimilation–double edged, at once subversive and affirming. Metonymically, it offers a pointed analogue for the relationship connecting *Night Cries* to mainstream cinema.

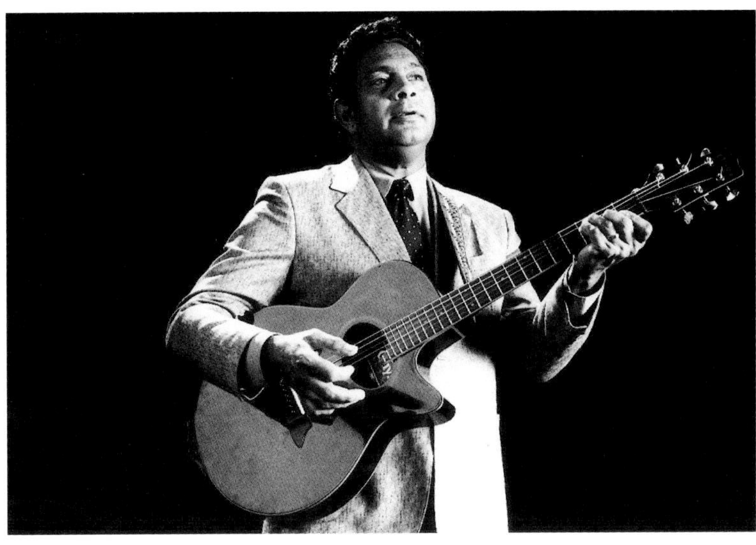

still from *Night Cries: A Rural Tragedy*, 1989

By using Little to frame and fragment the dominant narrative, Moffatt also problematizes the charged emotional register of the parental relationship. Abruptly interrupting the narrative's linearity, the saccharine lyrics, plangent strains, and manufactured sensations, endemic to pop songs in general and a feature of this one in particular, offer hollow comfort at the same time as they preclude the possibility of any direct emotional identification with either of the principals. In preventing this cathartic accord, *Night Cries* resurrects other feelings, such as fear, which linger uneasily in the Australian imaginary. Jean Genet acutely defined their source when he argued that "the difference between whites and blacks today lies less in skin color or the kind of hair than in their minds haunted by fears."[4] Moffatt astutely builds on this recognition, contrasting the girl's horror of abandonment by her mother (which appears as a recurrent nightmare) with the more vigorously repressed anxieties experienced by a white society concerning the minority race it has attempted both to adopt and to defranchise. The foundation of most interracial relationships in Australia lies in surrogate parenting: until the seventies, it was official government policy to remove Aboriginal children from their natural parents and place them with foster white families or in orphanages, a policy that had assimilation as its stated aim but genocide its likely result. Marcia Langton, the actress who plays the daughter in Moffatt's film, contends: "Perhaps the worst nightmare of the adoptive parents is to end life with the black adoptive child as the only family, the only one who cares."[5] Such fears are deeply buried within the collective imaginary of white

still from Charles Chauvel's *Jedda*, 1956

3
Homi Bhabha, "Of Mimicry and Man: The Ambivalence of Colonial Discourse," *October*, no. 28 (Spring 1984), p. 126.

4
Jean Genet, *Un captif amoureux* (1986), quoted in Catherine David, "Recent Ruins," in *Robert Gober* (Paris: Galerie Nationale du Jeu de Paume, 1991), p. 86.

5
Quoted in Patricia Mellencamp, "Haunted History: Tracey Moffatt and Julie Dash," *Discourse* 16, no. 2 (Winter 1993/94), p. 142.

Australia. Thus while *Night Cries* may be read as a powerful evocation of a paradigmatic relationship, it can equally be taken as an examination of a particular societal, as well as an individual, filiation, "unnatural" yet intensely charged.

Moffatt's work has also been interpreted as a pointed critique of traditional ethnographic film, which typically addressed Aboriginal issues through the idioms and conventions particular to naturalistic documentary film and photography.[6] Recognizing both the constructed nature of the fundaments of anthropological practice and the impossibility of portraying through the camera a reality that is inherently fictional, ethnography has recently focused on redefining the traditional relationship between the anthropologist and the object of study, and on exploring recording techniques that address the limitations and presuppositions integral to representation itself. Paralleling some of these more innovative current practices, Moffatt's synthetic approach also owes much to its roots in fine-art practices of the eighties.[7] Like many of her peers who came to maturity in the later part of that decade, she eschewed straight photography in favor of staged and fictive representations. While also informed loosely by cultural theory, her art is far from didactic or doctrinaire, and can never be reduced to a feminist or ethnic polemic. Welding tropes from painting, film, theater, and photography into a patently hybrid entity, her nuanced heteroglot style speaks to the complexity of a postcolonial society in which mixed-race relationships, such as this between mother and daughter, cannot be approached as already known, as preordained. By not reproducing reality, that is, by not *taking* pictures but by *making* pictures, Moffatt suggests metaphorically that such relationships in their specificity are not given but must be constructed—created, literally, from the shards of older stereotypes.

Since the relationship of *Something More* to its prototype was one of quotation and appropriation rather than of redeployment, Moffatt reinforced its stereotypes as not only formulaic but fixed, as if they were mythic in essence and, consequently, uninflected by or indifferent to race, region, and historical circumstance. *Night Cries*, on the other hand, by means of a series of condensations and displacements, invalidates the premises of the perennial debate between biological determinism and cultural conditioning, reconfiguring that antithesis to stress the crucial roles of the historical moment and cultural context in defining, molding, and governing identity. Unlike its fifties' predecessor, which might best be classified as mainstream entertainment, *Night Cries* invests this subject with a socio-mythological import at the same time as it raises emphatically the question of history.

In the years immediately following her acclaimed debut, Moffatt's strongest work allied itself more closely and narrowly than previously with photographic modes, though she continued to work in the manner of a film director, with hired

6
Comparison might also be made with *Some Lads* (1986), her earliest series, which was made in part as a critique of stereotypical nineteenth-century portrayals of Aborigines, such as those by J. W. Lindt. Comprised of six black-and-white photographs, it takes as its subject several young male dancers, all of whom are of Aboriginal or mixed-race background. In place of traditional, hence tribal, dance, Moffatt focuses on men trained in the techniques of modern dance or ballet in order to create seductive images that treat the subjects neither as primitives nor as objects of desire, nor as effeminate—all conventional stereotypes that surround this charged theme. The results are documentary-style studio shots in which the subjects, well aware of the camera, are set against paint-splattered backcloths in a playful reference to fine art via Jackson Pollock as well as to its

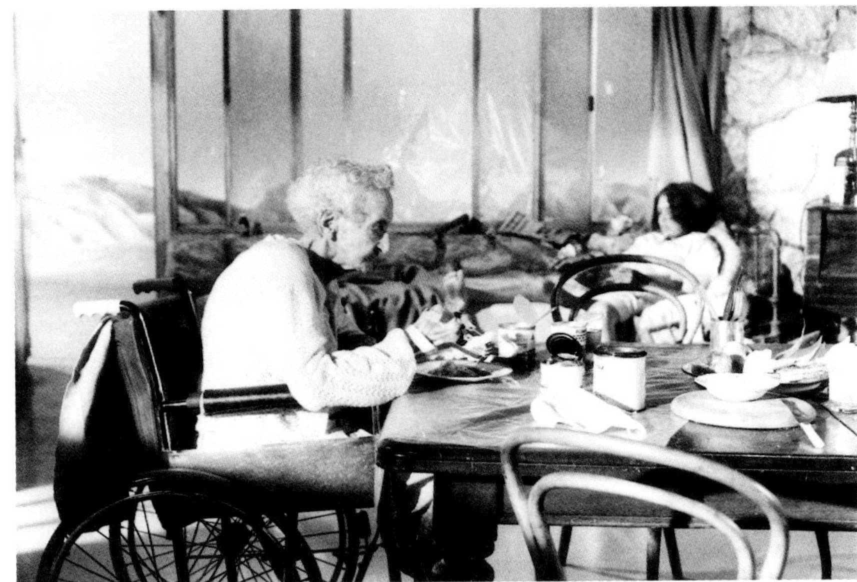

still from *Night Cries: A Rural Tragedy*, 1989

actors, props, and a camera crew. As before, the possibility of a potent reinscription of the known into local dialect proved more compelling than a search for innovative or original inscriptions *tout court*. *Pet Thang* (1991), a phototableau, seems initially to be a reworking of a fairly obvious trope based on the dialectical relationship between the narcissism of the centerfold and the masculinity of the gaze, here underscored by the sumptuous production values. Moreover, since issues of race are often interwoven with those of gender in any multiethnic society, they too are inevitably encoded within this starkly pared opposition of sex object and animal. "Pet" is an epithet frequently used in Australian jargon to indicate endearment and approval toward children. When applied to women, it becomes as patronizing and fetishizing as its near counterpart "doll." The subtext that informs this photo series is also rooted in language, in the commonplace if contentious assertion that Australia grew to nationhood on the back of its sheep. The claim is closely allied to that which maintains Australia was an empty land, a terra nullius, until its annexation by Europeans in the eighteenth century. Ignoring the long presence of Aboriginal societies, such beliefs deny the contribution of the continent's first inhabitants to its history as well as its contemporary culture.

The opening shot in the series foregrounds in hallucinatory intensity the large head of a sheep. Subsequent photographs establish an opposition between the female figure—again played by Moffatt herself—and the ewe, each floating, fragmented, in a darkened and dimensionless space. The kindred

commercial counterpart, house painting. The straightforwardness of the shot, together with the heightened detail, impute an objectivity to the image, treating the medium as a vehicle for the dancers to comment or present themselves as themselves rather than as actors within a fictive world, which has been the case in all of Moffatt's subsequent work. Thus, exceptionally in her oeuvre, reality is here constituted by the photographic image. Since in contemporary society this is increasingly the image of advertising and consumption, it is fitting that these "lads" should have affinities with their kin in pictures promoting Gap and Calvin Klein apparel.

7
For a fuller discussion see Gael Newton, "Tracey Moffatt: Cover Girl," in *Tracey Moffatt: Fever Pitch* (Annandale, Australia: Piper Press, 1995), pp.13–22.

nature of the female figure and the animal as both objects of desire and as signifiers of possession and power is reinforced later in the series when the female nude is paired with a lamb, a conventional symbol for the sacrificial victim. The final plate reverts to a close-up, this time of the woman's head, eyes closed, withdrawn, passive, object as much as subject. The blurring and fragmenting of these motifs not only enhance the oneiric mood but fetishize the images, just as the lurid tonality gives a superficial surface identity to the more fundamental analogies lampooned in this work. Echoing the lyrics of a crass country-and-western song, the title introjects a jarring tone, mocking the seamless complicity between exhibitionism and voyeurism on which this work's schlock precedents depend.

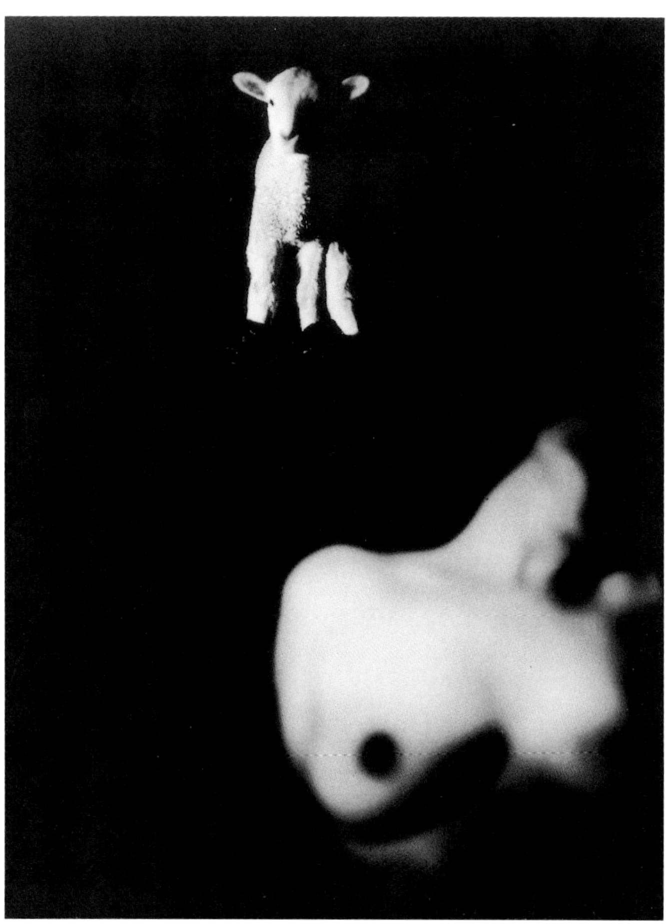

from *Pet Thang*, 1991

Scarred for Life, Moffatt's next series, again draws on photography's popular history rather than its fine-art traditions, partly because it adopts a form akin to that of a poster. Printed in a large edition, each part was originally intended to be pinned directly to the wall. Despite the fact that its prototypes, derived from *Life* magazine layouts from the thirties, are coded as documentary, this series again employs staged photography. Accompanied by pithy captions, these anecdotal images embody the conflict endemic to familial relationships in terse but telling vignettes. Rare in Moffatt's work, each of these scenes is autonomous, so a metanarrative neither links individual parts nor determines sequence. Vernacular detail from suburban sixties' Australia gives eloquent texture to scenes and situations that, for the first time in Moffatt's oeuvre, have been divested of both an exclusive and a critical relationship to any particular place and culture. Though these episodes are manifestly located within a multiracial society, ethnic diversity is now treated not as a subject but as a precondition of contemporary life.

Incidents based in childhood or adolescent experiences form the basis of this anthology. Though their tone is retrospective, nostalgia and sentiment are rejected. While the appending of such a title to familiar and apparently mundane events may initially appear facetious, it soon reveals itself as ominously freighted with the ring of truth, hence whatever humor they generate is invariably acerbic. Marking abrupt and painful entries into adulthood, these moments have branded themselves indelibly in their subjects' psyches: they were nothing less than rites of passage.

Despite this widening of reference, Moffatt's work continued to be grounded in childhood memories, experiences that are as likely to have had their sources in the mass media as in actuality, and hence in imported cultures as well as vernacular ones. *GUAPA (Good Looking)*, the series she produced in 1995 while on a residency in San Antonio, Texas, originated in memories of televised roller derby contests, which she avidly watched as an adolescent growing up in Mt. Gravatt, a working-class suburb of Brisbane. Fascinated by the faked violence and erotic posturing, trademarks of this ersatz sport, she reconstructed it primarily as a vehicle to reprise the theme of female rivalry. Unlike mainstream sports, which are traditionally seen to offer black youth a way out of the ghetto, the roller derby offered no such escape routes for women. As evidenced by Moffatt's contenders, whose bodies bear little trace of rigorous training and whose costumes owe as much to a grunge aesthetic as to functional considerations, this competition was a site for camp entertainment rather than displays of skill or prowess. The faux primitive body-paint, like the machismo posturing, serves primarily to eroticize and dramatize what, in her evocation as in reality, are little more than spectacles of licensed sexual aggression. To reinforce this reading, she also dispensed with a background, suspending her contestants' encounters in an abstracted realm. By printing the final images in a soft magenta hue, she further suppressed detail, anecdotal immediacy, and stark physicality, thereby reinforcing the overriding impression of choreographed motion: description gives way to calligraphy in these unblushingly aestheticized staged simulations.

If many of *GUAPA*'s ten images insistently recall Maya Deren's seminal forties' films of dancers, or Rodin's studies of lissome performers in action, they equally have their roots in the familiar lexicon of sports photojournalism. Privileging typical moments or incidents from within a standardized repertoire, this genre crystallizes split-second actions into striking formal compositions. Moffatt's frumpy protagonists vividly silhouetted in limbo fit comfortably within this genre. Although linked in a quasi narrative, which functions primarily as a casual vehicle for ordering the sequence, these images retain an autonomy comparable to that found in celebrated sports photographs and in artworks alike. By weaving references from commercial and fine-art traditions, Moffatt posits certain parallels in the functions of sport and art: both conventionalize into decorous and approved modes impulses that are otherwise perceived as primal, hence, socially unacceptable.

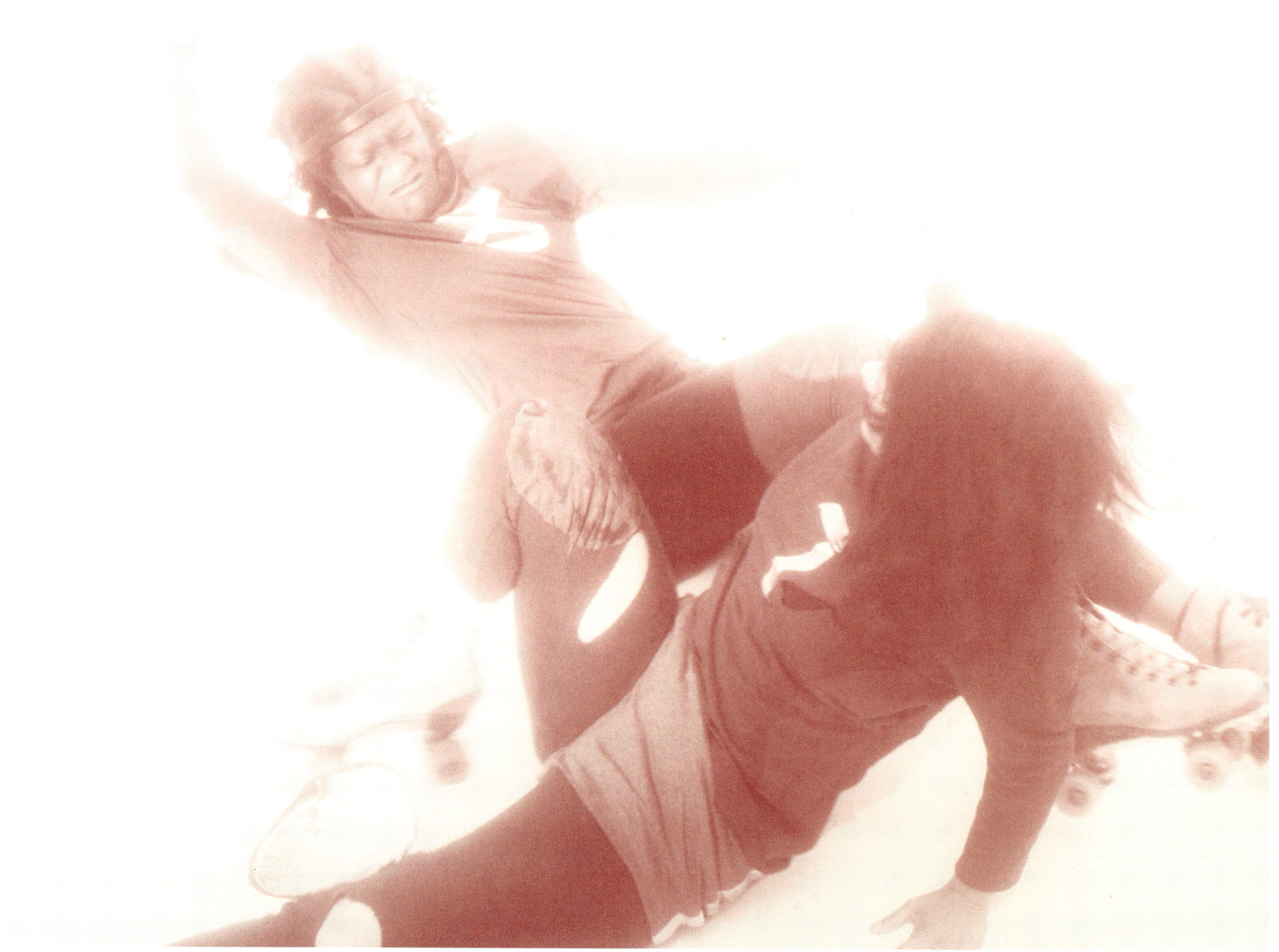

from *GUAPA (Good Looking)*, 1995

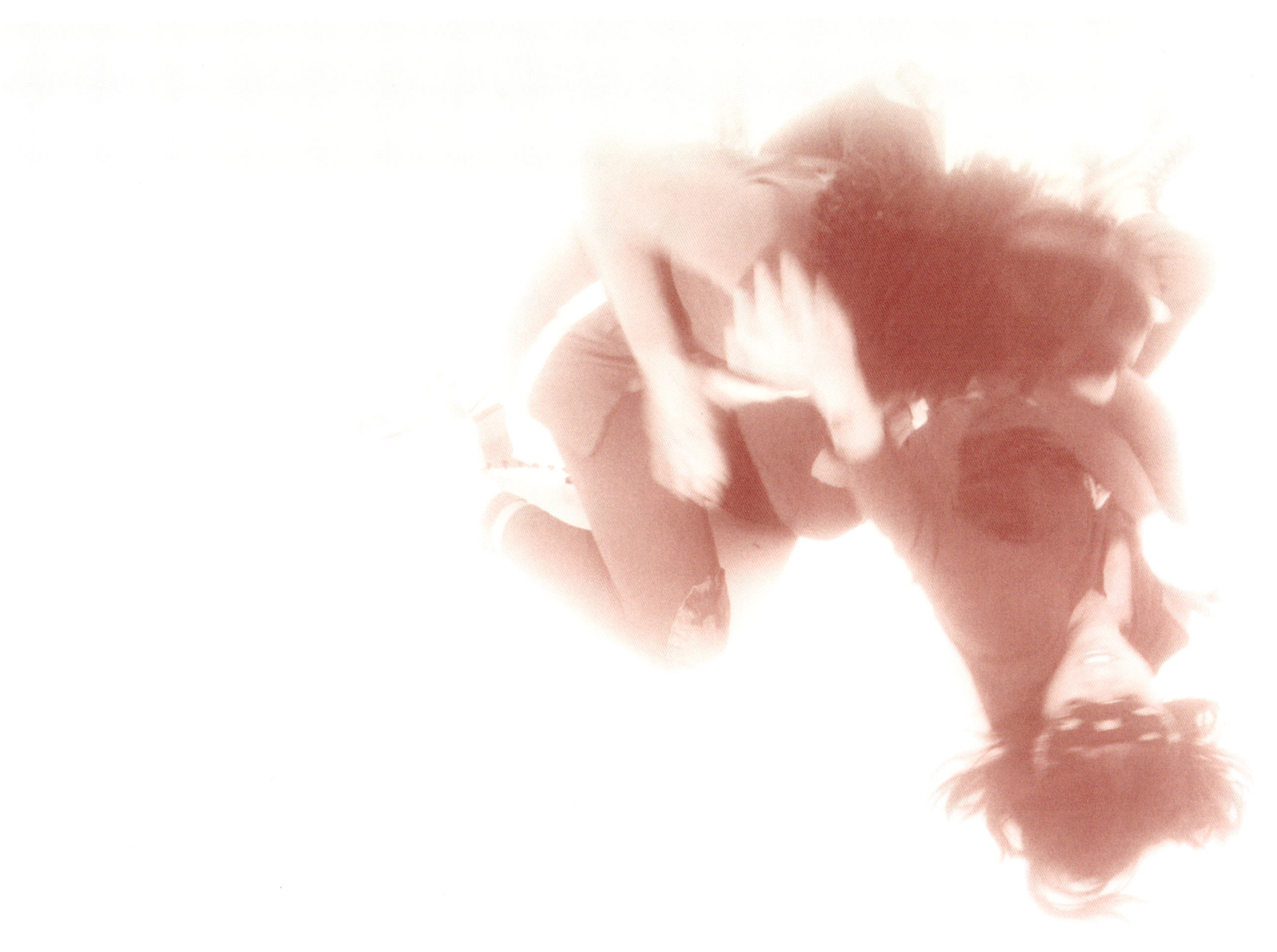

Up in the Sky (1997), Moffatt's latest and largest photo series to date, is also her most complex and sophisticated in its manipulation of the dual languages and histories of film and photography. Shooting outdoors on location, Moffatt for the first time dispensed with scenography, and hence with landscape as a backdrop, as well as with allusions and methods drawn from painting. Hinged around a triangular love relationship that also involves issues of paternity, *Up in the Sky* introduces numerous subsidiary characters in scenes that are imbued only rarely with the degree of artifice–the staged quality–that characterized her earlier work. Photographing on location in daylight produces a flattening effect that not only tends to fuse her subjects into an ensemble aligned on a single plane, but welds them indissolubly to their milieu.

Starting within a decrepit bungalow housing a white woman and a black baby, the settings rapidly move outside to reveal a shantytown sprawling over flat terrain. Beyond, even more barren desert reaches are crisscrossed by monumental embankments of elevated highways and littered with abandoned vehicles. A place of ruin more than of uncharted frontier, this is home to a trove of social misfits, to white trash as well as deracinated Aborigines. In this radically revised version of the West/Outback, Moffatt, in characteristic fashion, reverses roles so that her car-wreckers/salvagers are muscular women, tough female successors to Mad Max's hooligans. Likewise, what were formerly epic fights between archetypal heroes are reduced to mere skirmishes in the dust between black and white youths brandishing nothing more lethal than a pocketknife. Notwithstanding the softened focus and monochromatic tonality in which each image has been printed, this is no lost Eden: anarchy lurks just below the surface in this liminal dystopia.

Like *Night Cries*, *Up in the Sky* is closely linked to a preexisting work, in this case to Pier Paolo Pasolini's masterpiece of Italian neorealist cinema, *Accattone* (1961). Basing her episodes in large part on incidents within Pasolini's narrative, sharing his preference for street actors over professionals, and structuring many of her shots in memory of his, Moffatt, like her mentor, evolves a form of realism that refutes naturalism. Yet in reprising his world of social marginals, Moffatt, not surprisingly, substitutes the mother-whore for his pimps. Her chief protagonist thus becomes a pregnant woman, her figures of institutional authority nuns, and her workers auto predators. In switching her focus from one gender to another, Moffatt undermines the mockery implicit in the refrain sung jestingly by one of Pasolini's men about his "meal ticket," turning the implication of the phrase "up in the sky," which she adopts as her title, from denigration to approbation. The last photograph in the series depicts the young Aboriginal suitor (father?) as a tiny figure dwarfed by the parched rolling hills. In contrast to that of his forbear in Pasolini's film, an unmitigated solitariness, not death, is his destiny. Given that Moffatt's ambiguously ironic pastiche is not shorn of pathos, it recalls the recent fiction of Sam Shepard and other devotees of the contemporary

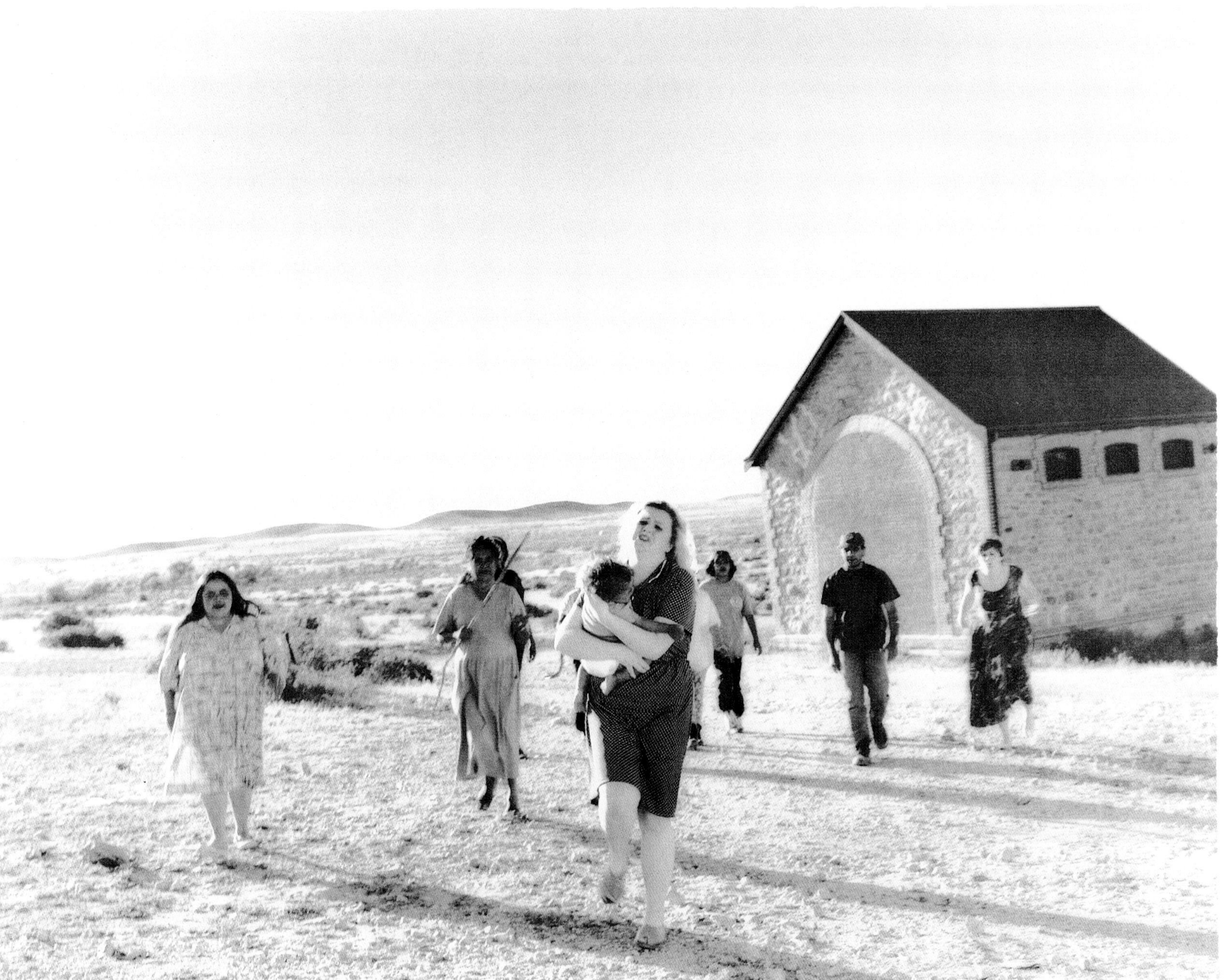

from *Up in the Sky*, 1997

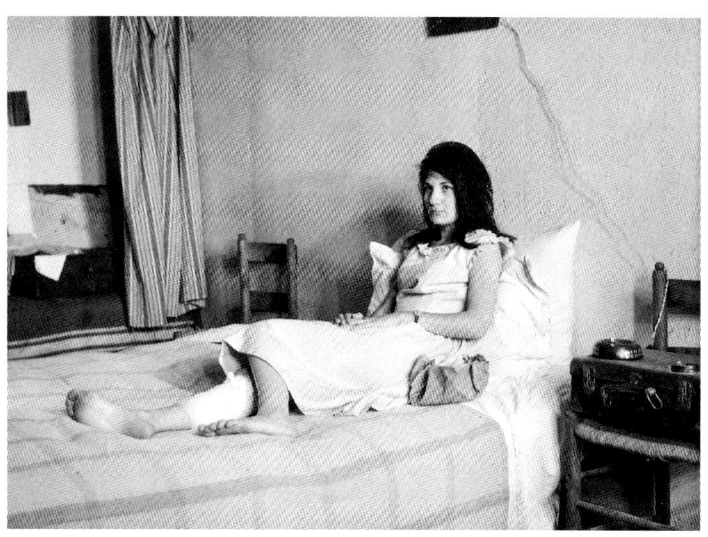

still from Pier Paolo Pasolini's *Accattone*, 1961

American West. Where the West (Outback) was formerly constructed in terms of archetypes and as a site of the mythic, these contemporary rewritings present it as ineluctably subject to the historicity of representation. Consequently, what formerly was parsed as alienation now takes on another coloration. Étienne Balibar persuasively argues that contemporary society has "moved from the thematics of alienation to the thematics of alterity; the sign has been reversed. It is no longer a question of alienating oneself or overcoming one's alienation," he contends, "but instead of knowing what one makes of alterity."[8] In the mixed-race society of *Up in the Sky*, race relations per se are not the issue, alterity has multiple referents, multiple castes.

Counterpointing the oneiric existentialism that is the fate of the lone male, a sense of community—albeit a fragile and provisional one—coheres around the woman and child, who are always depicted as socialized, integrated as opposed to marginalized. If Shepard's fiction explodes the myth of the West to demonstrate that it lives on only in the imaginary, as an existentialism available only via reverie, Pasolini's oeuvre is branded with the conviction that entry into the social order is the equivalent of death. Equivocating between these related visions, *Up in the Sky* presents its chief protagonists as ultimately trapped in the antimony between the universal and the historical, the condition and the conditioned, the transcendental and the empirico-historical.

The linear narrative of *Accattone* automatically becomes more elliptical when translated into the static medium of photography, but Moffatt renders it more disjunctive by her treatment of character and, above all, space and place. Her protagonists, too, remain strangely impersonal, aloof even in close-up, but, in contrast to the Italian's, her miscellaneous vistas resist being reconciled into a single location. The discontinuity of the pictorial space precludes the positing of a unitary, coherent identity to this terrain, which becomes a social space where people seem inadvertently to have ended up, as distinct from a desired destination. Not no-where in that it is a place marked by particularity even if divested of identity, this alienated nonplace is a heterotopic space, a space that has lost its homogeneity and forfeited its systems of interconnections. Linkages here depend on movements of affectivity, on attempts to group and unite—to act collectively—irrespective of how limited, tentative, contingent, and temporary such attempts must inevitably prove.

8
Étienne Balibar, "Globalization/Civilization 1," in conversation with Jean-François Chevrier, Catherine David, and Nadia Tazi, in *Politics-Poetics: documenta x—The Book* (Ostfildern-Ruit, Germany: Cantz, 1997), p. 783.

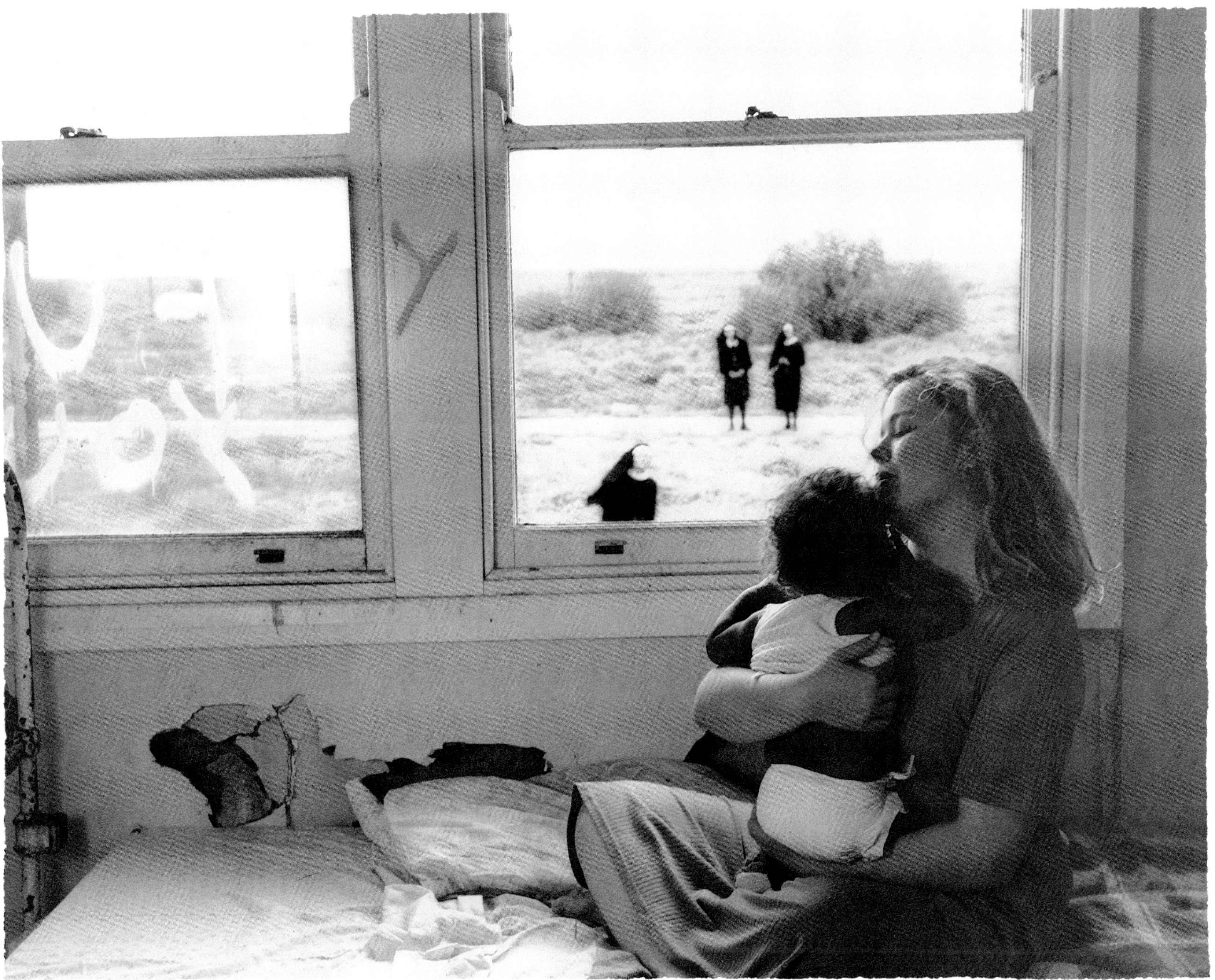

from *Up in the Sky*, 1997

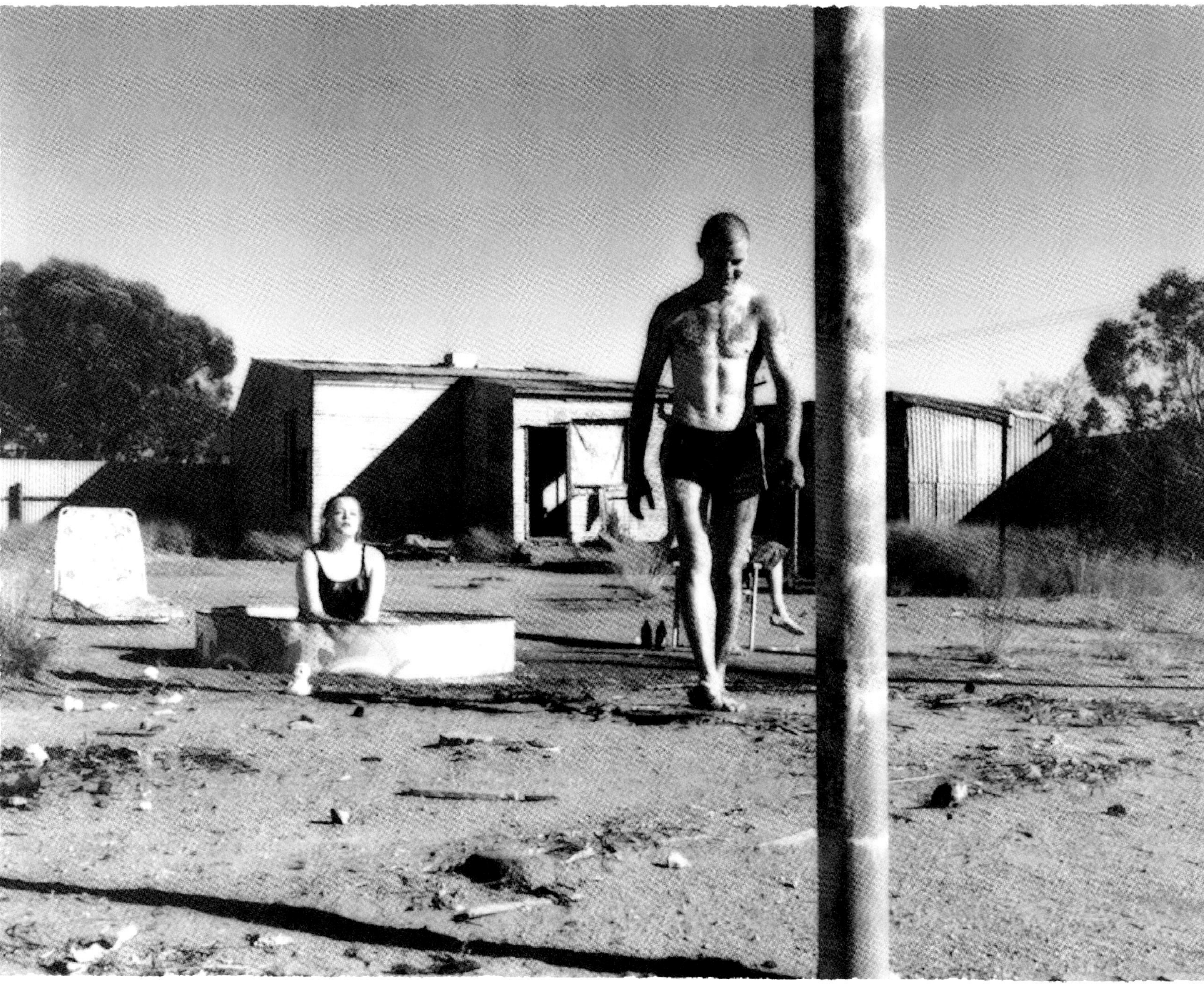

from *Up in the Sky*, 1997

The majority of divergent allusions that make *Up in the Sky* so visually rich are derived from cinema, from both its commercial and fine-art modes.[9] Formally, Moffatt also plays with standard cinematic techniques. Images in this series, in particular, seem filmic in that, however elusive the narrative, their unfolding is more important than the link each has to its referent, whereas the opposite is the case with still photography, in which the individual representation typically appears more tightly tied indexically to its source, to what was but no longer is. This cinematic effect is reinforced by the slightly fuzzy quality of the printing, which divests the motifs of the precise definition that in photography conventionally stresses its indexicality, its specificity and actuality. On occasion, Moffatt puts illusionism further into question in what is becoming a more subtle language of self-disclosing artifice in comparison with her former highly stylized idiom. For example, in several images the bystanders bemusedly look directly at the camera, and hence to the very place occupied by the viewer. Elsewhere, the ground is arbitrarily and vertiginously tilted as if to correspond to a player's point of view but the subject is never identified. Or, a medium shot of a scene of the mother bathing in a child's wading pool is unaccountably bisected by a foregrounded pole. This rephrasing of standard cinematic camera angles or setups disorients and destabilizes, underlining Moffatt's characterization of this location as a social limbo, and, consequently, reinstating her burgeoning preference for the conjectural over closure.

The larger canvas limned in *Up in the Sky* has an epic quality new to Moffatt's oeuvre. Overlaying the photographic and filmic, and mass-cultural as well as high-art idioms, Moffatt has developed a synthetic polyglot style, which is at once referentially apposite and finely attuned technically for probing the complex relations between the ontological condition and the sociohistorical. By the artist's own account, her prime motivation is a desire for images.[10] As a survey of her art over the past decade reveals, this voracious appetite purloins a compendious farrago of media, modes, and norms of representation. Certain subjects or stories, usually stemming from childhood, act as catalysts. While originating in personal experience, they are never confined to the autobiographical, but depend upon the realm of collective memory. The heterogeneous borrowings, quotations, and parodic rewritings in which they are manifest reinforce this locus in the contemporary imaginary. For although Moffatt, like Pasolini, is a pasticheur as much by passion as by calculation, her subject is ultimately, and always, the historicity of representation.

9
In addition to *Accattone*, other works by Pasolini, most notably *Oedipus Rex* (1967), are particularly relevant to this analysis.

10
See Tracey Moffatt, "Fever Pitch," in *Tracey Moffatt: Fever Pitch*, pp.5–6.

Up in the Sky, 1997

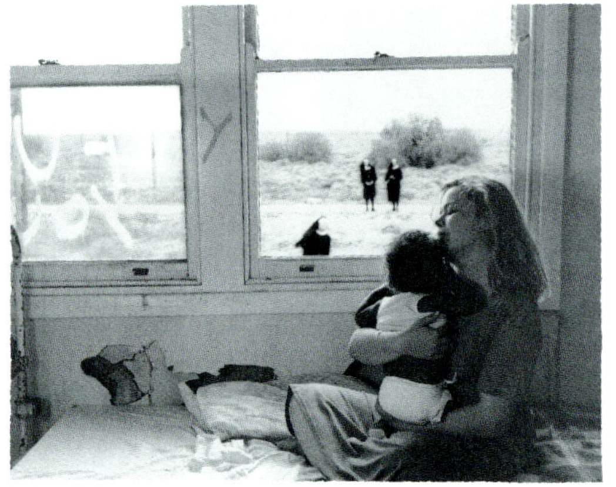

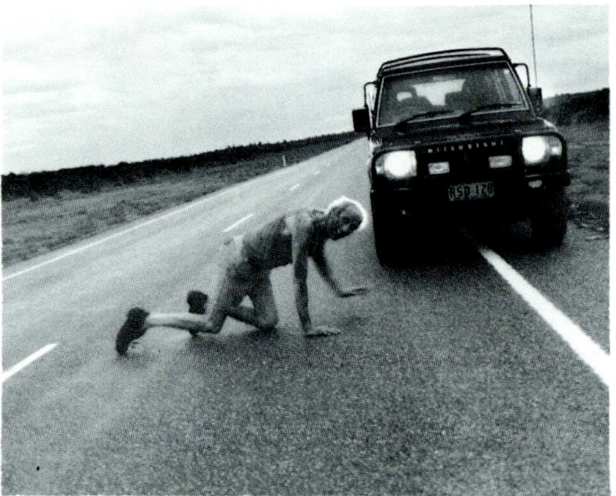

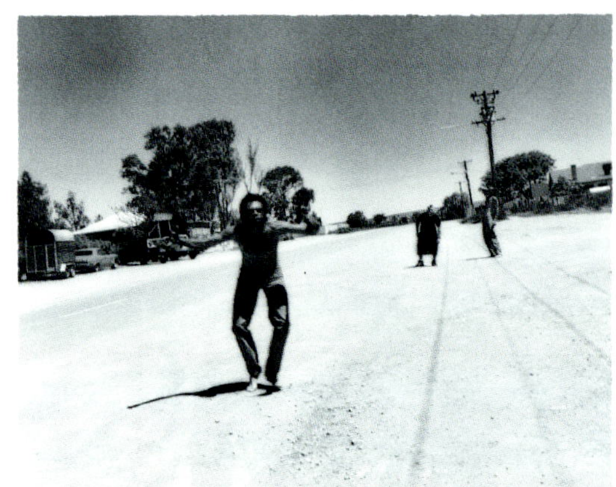

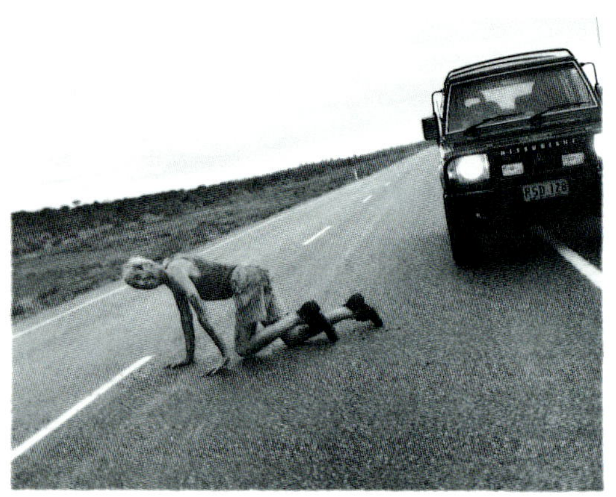

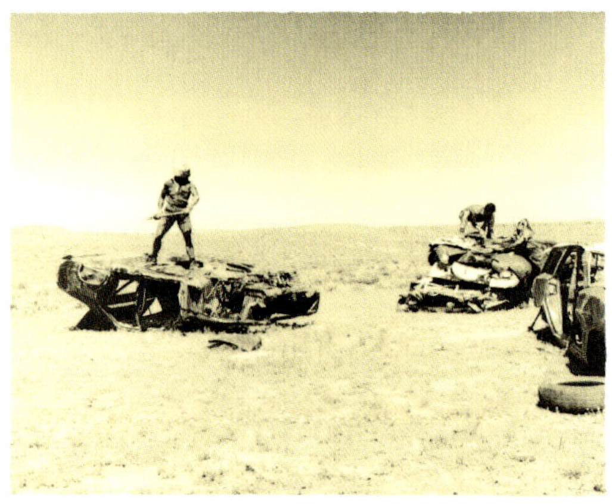

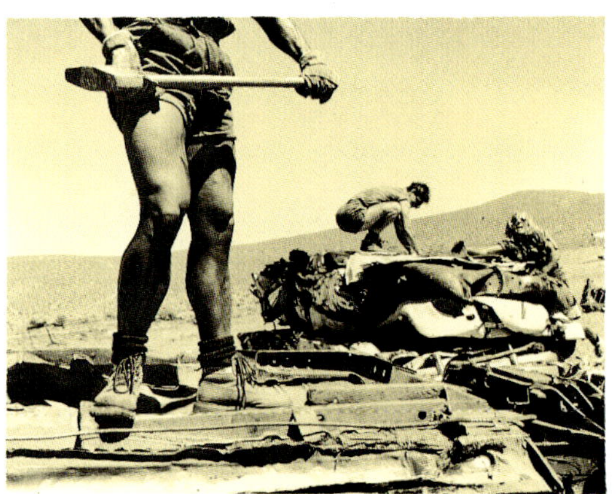

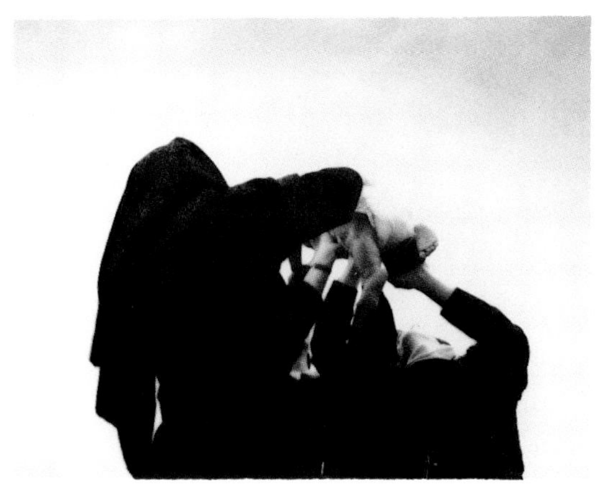
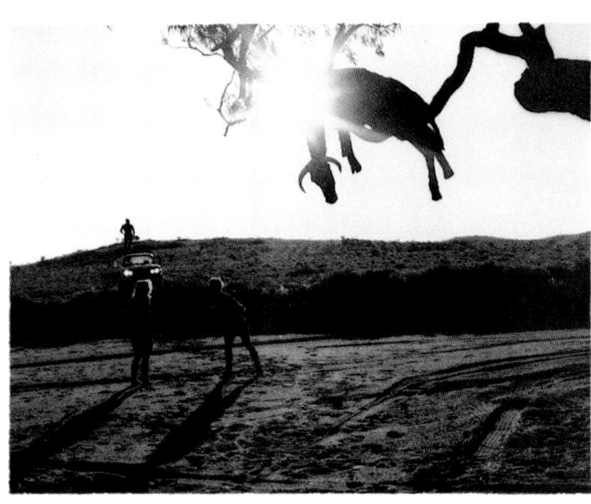
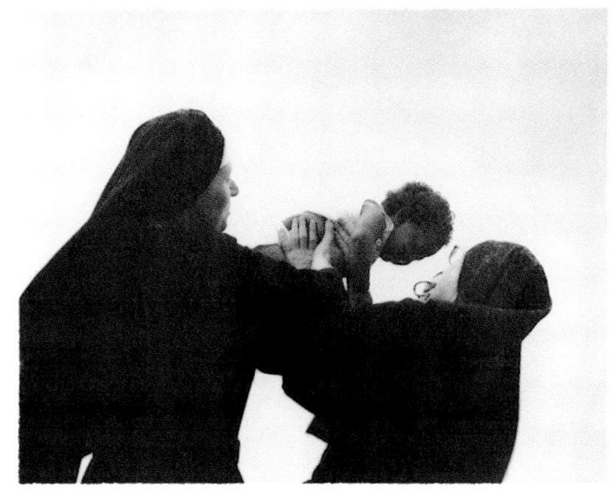
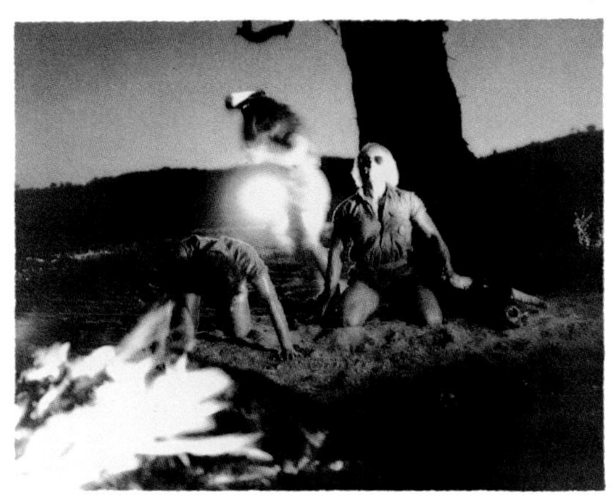
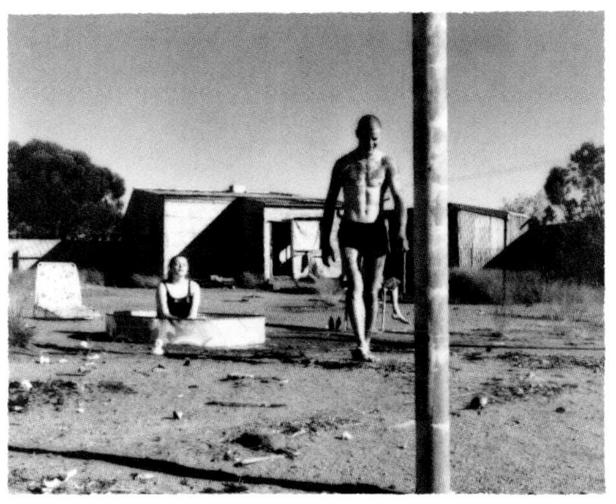
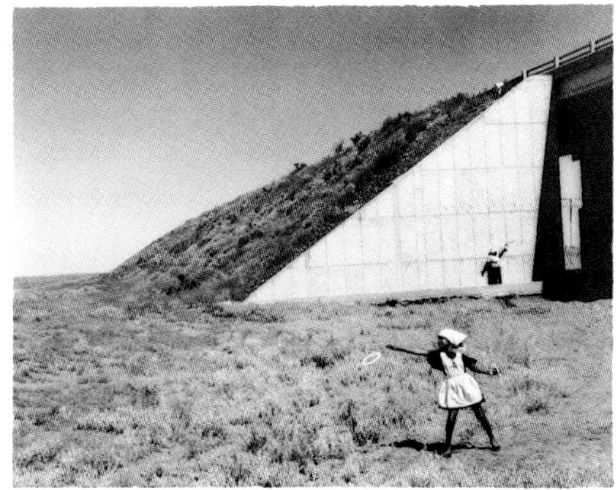

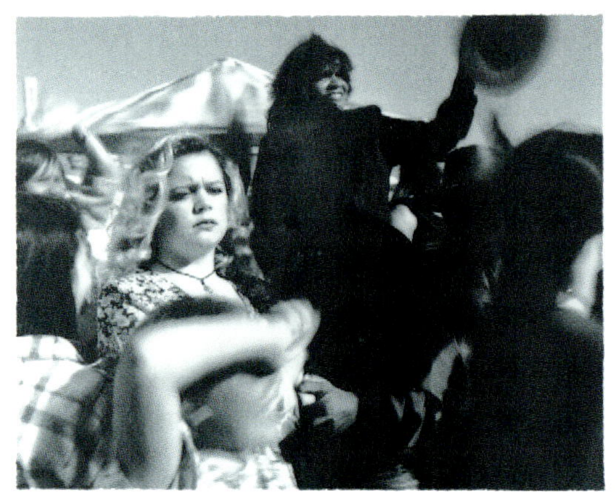
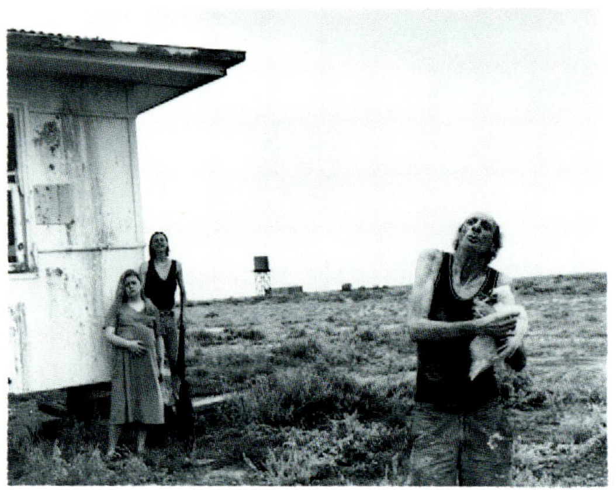
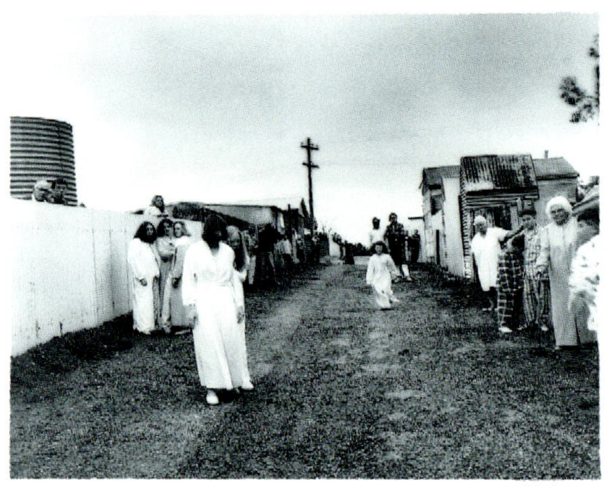
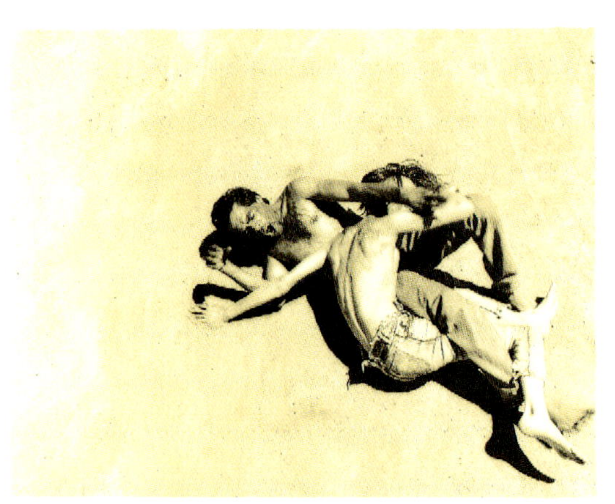
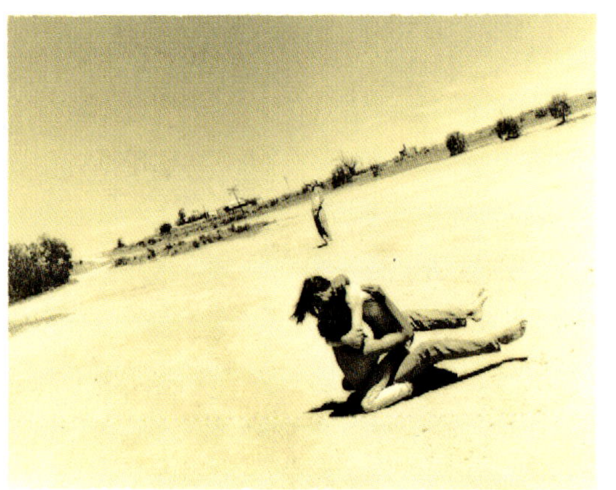
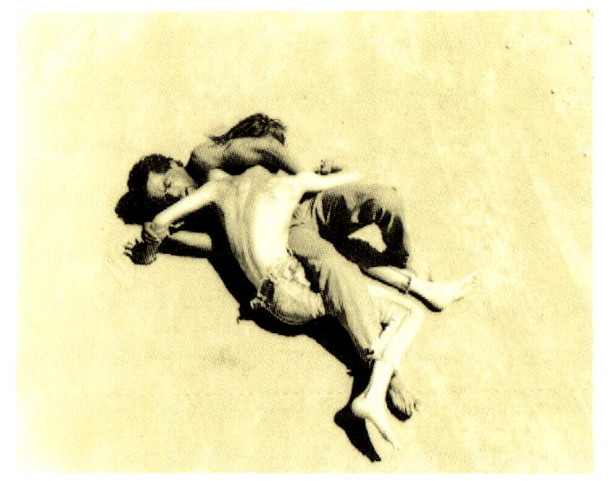

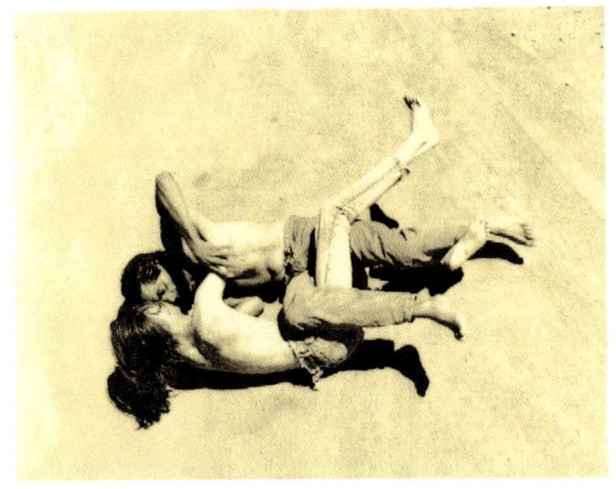

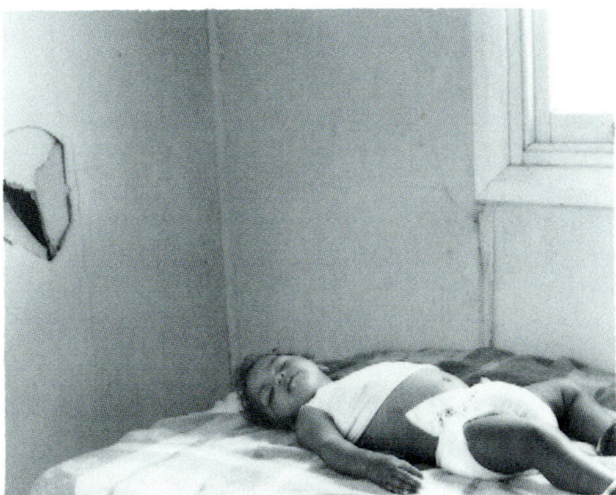

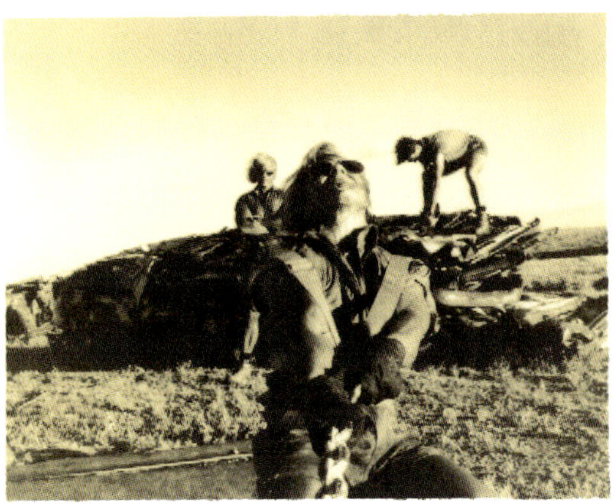

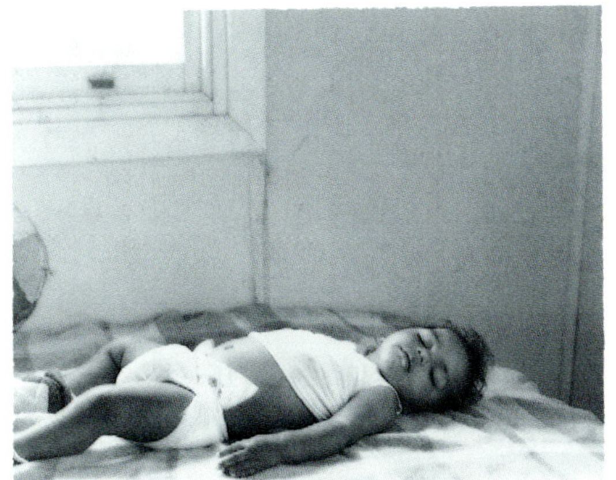

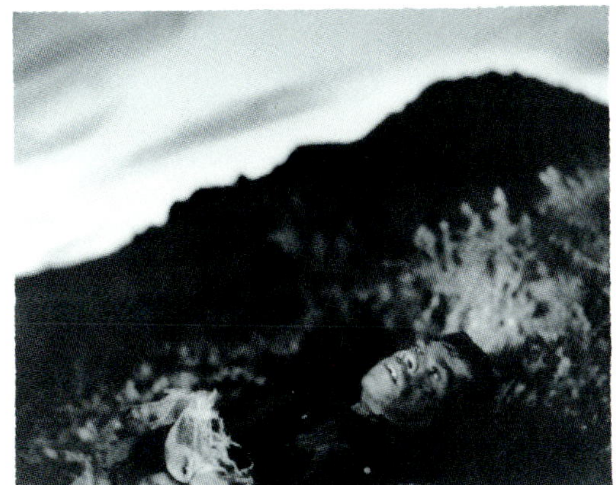

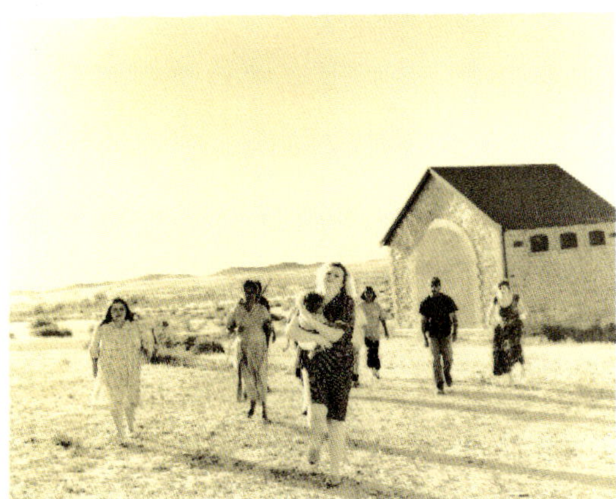

overleaf: final image from *Up in the Sky*

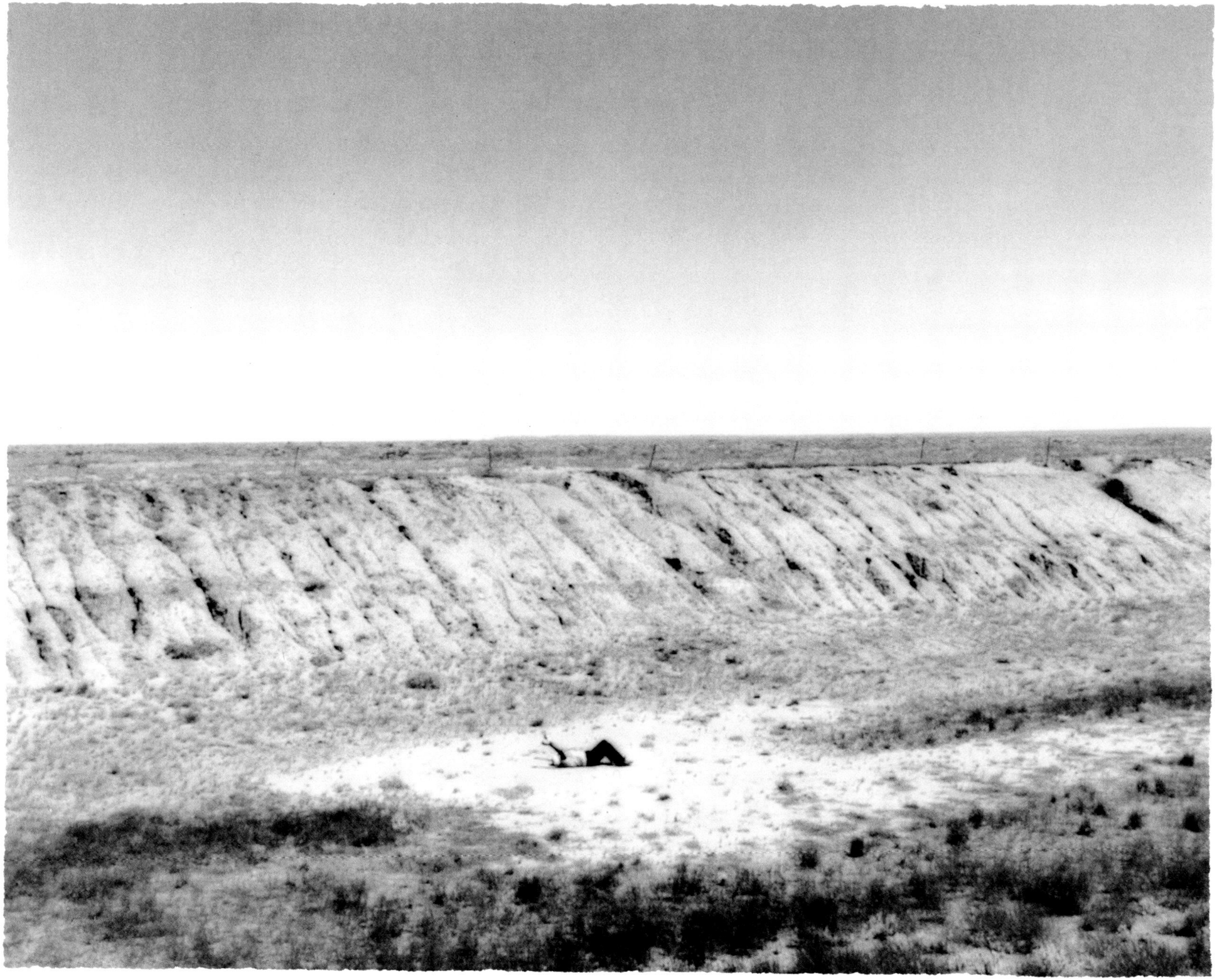

Dust

Sam Shepard

Price crept slowly into town, passing a little landmark sign that read: *Belvidere–The Town Too Tough To Die*. He didn't see any town to speak of. An abandoned tire repair shop. An abandoned barbecue joint called Tibbs' Ribs. The only thing not abandoned was a Conoco station with a little café and food shop behind it. He pulled in there and parked. It was still too early for Lowell and his fabulous daughter to show up. The only thing he could remember him saying about the meeting place was the Belvidere turnoff. So this was good enough. He could see the highway exit from where he sat. He watched some aging bikers roll into the parking lot, riding double on giant Jap bikes with little microphones implanted in their helmets, like fat Martians. Their lips were moving, but he couldn't hear any voices. Whatever happened to *The Fugitive Kind*? he wondered. At least they *belong* to something; some Japanese biker world for fatties. He pulled himself up on the seat and started having second thoughts about this meeting. After all, the only real reason he'd come was just to catch another glimpse of Lowell's daughter. He felt a little guilty about it. As he stuck the key in the ignition, he saw Lowell Hewitt's outfit crest a hill and cross the railroad tracks, heading for the Conoco station. Although Price had never seen Lowell's truck and trailer before, he knew it had to be him. The pickup was an extension of Lowell himself, an old green Ford Ranger so layered in prairie dust and gumbo mud that it had become part of the paint job itself. There weren't two matching tires on the entire rig, including the stock trailer, which was a battered flesh color scarred with huge liver-shaped rust spots dotting the nose and fenders. Three saddled ranch horses were frantically clawing to catch their balance as Lowell fishtailed the trailer into the gas station and slammed on brakes, sending the horses crashing forward, almost to their knees. "Had yer breakfast yet!" Lowell yelled out the window at him, through the settling dust.

"Yessir!" Price called back, pulling the keys out of the ignition. Madilia's raw face was hidden behind her father's hat brim, but Price caught a glimpse of her, slamming her shoulder into the jammed door on her side, trying to bail out. His heart clicked in his throat.

"That's good, 'cause we won't eat again till sundown! Some fancy outfits hire a Piper Cub to drop lunch, but we're not one of those! Never have been." Lowell laughed and hawked a rolling gob of tobacco juice in Price's direction as he headed across the gravel toward them. Madilia finally got her door punched open and went around the tailgate of the pickup and hopped the hitch. He was hoping she'd at least take a look at him, but she just strode straight off toward the café, with her hands stuffed in her back pockets. He felt like teenager, the way his head was heating up. "Why don't you pile on in with us, Price? No point takin' two vehicles back in there."

"No, that's all right. I'll just follow."

"Suit yerself. Yer gonna eat a lotta dust, though. These old washboard roads can really kick it up."

"That's okay. Doesn't look like you've got much room in there."

"How much room do ya need?" Lowell jeered, spewing brown Copenhagen slime again. There was an awkward pause where Price found himself turning back toward the little café in anticipation of Madilia's return. He felt caught now and almost wished he were a member of the fat-biker group, waddling off toward their glitzy machines, sucking on gonzo Pepsis. He turned back to Lowell and made a faint attempt at a smile.

"You brought an extra horse, huh?" he said to Lowell.

"You didn't wanna ride double, did ya? Or maybe you did!" Lowell reached out the window of the truck and punched Price's shoulder, then guffawed and pounded on the steering wheel with his other hand. "That old high cantle she rides'll knock yer dick in the dirt!" He launched into a hacking and spitting fit, while Price rubbed his shoulder, hoping Lowell wouldn't notice that his punch had actually gotten to him a bit. "You don't wanna mess around with any half-breed women anyhow, Price. Believe you me. They'll eat yer lunch!"

"Why's that?"

"Just lead to big trouble for ya back there in Ioway. Besides, yer married, ain't ya?"

"I'm not from Iowa," Price said, and he looked up right into Lowell's wide face. Lowell stopped gnawing on his chew and stared at him blankly.

"Thought you said you was from Iowa, or was I half in the bag?"

"Yeah, that's what I said, but I'm not from there. I don't like Iowa—especially Des Moines. Des Moines reminds me of Russia."

"Well, where the heck are ya from, then?"

"Kentucky," Price said off the top of his head.

"I'll be darned. Kentucky. Suppose yer not in the fertilizer business either."

"That's right. I'm not."

"I'll be doggoned. How 'bout the married part? Yer not makin' that up, are ya, or am I a complete fool?"

"No. That part's true."

"Well, least we got half a leg to stand on." Lowell took a long, hard look at Price, then smiled and spit the whole used-up wad of Copenhagen out the window and watched it land like a steaming turd. "Yer one mixed-up fella, ain't ya, Price?"

Madilia came out of the café, swinging a six-pack of Budweiser in each hand and walking just like Price imagined she would. She didn't smile at him until she got within a few yards of the truck. "You comin' with us in our outfit?" she asked him as she kept right on striding around to her door.

"No, I'm going to follow."

"Yer liable to eat a lotta dust."

"That's what your dad told me."

"He was right," she said, just before she slammed the creaking door.

Price tried to keep up with Lowell's rig the best he could on the gravel ranch roads, but the closer he kept to the stock trailer, the less visibility he had through the swirling dust, until he was afraid he'd rear-end them if Lowell had to slam on brakes for some reason. He backed off a good eight or ten car lengths, but Lowell maintained a steady sixty, with the trailer wagging the dog through every turn and the horses scrambling to catch their feet. Price had known dust in his time, but this was beyond description. It poured through every possible crack, through the closed vent and the floorboards. He could taste it and grind it between his teeth. His nose and ears filled up with it. His eyes were caked with a gray crust. The back of his throat was coated with it. His hands turned pale and chalky. The narrow road snaked on and on, and all he could do was follow Lowell's storm and hope some John Deere hay wagon didn't suddenly poke up over a hill at 5 mph, heading in his direction. He began to feel a slight panic at the thought of losing this father-and-daughter team out here in the badlands. He had no clue where the interstate was now, and they'd already forked off at two or three different junctions. Junctions with no signposts or landmarks of any kind. He tried to remember which fork they'd just taken: the left or the right? Exactly how many? Two, he thought. Maybe three but most likely just two. Both to the left. He was almost sure they'd been both to the left. He started straining his eyes through the glass for some kind of distinguishing features, but the buttes in the distance all looked the same through the haze of dust. As soon as he'd fix on a unique, pyramid-shaped one—slate gray with salmon-colored stripes running horizontally through it—then another one would appear, identical to it. He fixed on one out his right window with a long, slender, wind-eroded neck and a knob on top that looked like a hawk's head. He thought *that* one would have to be singular and tried to memorize it as having been seen on his right, but then a twin to it suddenly appeared on his left. He thought he was in Egypt for a second. He saw buffalo turn into camels; shimmering heat bands on the horizon, with dark date palms suddenly jumping out and dancing in a line. All he could do was try to keep up. He accelerated three or four car lengths and resigned himself to the suffocating dust. The dashboard was so thick with it by now that he couldn't see the numbers on the speedometer. Not that speed mattered much. He began to imagine Lowell and his amazing daughter laughing their heads off at him and popping cans of Budweiser up ahead. He could almost see them elbowing each other in the ribs and punching the headliner. He wondered how it was that he'd suddenly become the object of ridicule in the middle of the open plains. His blood started to rise at the thought of it. It was women again. The stupid lure of women. He slammed the Buick down into second, causing the rear end to bite so violently he almost lost total control, but he pulled it back out and hugged the left shoulder. The dust attack was less on that side of the road, but the risk of a head-on slowly pushed him back over to the right again, directly on Lowell's tail. He stared into the jerry-rigged back gate of the horse trailer, a snarled-up network of old rotten ropes and baling wire lashing a slat-board gate in place. He was now face-to-face with the wild-eyed, spread-eagled horses, who had all turned tail and faced the rear, trying to avoid the relentless dust. A dun gelding, closest to the back gate, stared out at him, eyes terrified, nostrils pulsing for air. It was the stare of a plain victim.

After ten miles of this test by dust and gravel, they pulled off into a cedar brake, sheltering a jumble of ancient bleached-out corrals and loading chutes. Price parked by a stump and waited for them to emerge from the Ford. When he cut off the ignition, his body kept pulsing, as though the rutted road had somehow gotten up into his bones and would never leave him. He was chewing dirt and spitting whole gobs of it out the window. His lungs burned with it. He could see Madilia repeating the same madness of slamming her shoulder into the truck door. The violence of it, the way she committed her whole body to it, made him wonder how she could have ever had the power to draw him out this far into completely unknown territory. Her father swung his thick legs out. He was wearing the same indelible broad smile and squeezed a beer in his hand. "What kinda vehicle you call that, Price? Never seen anything like it!"

"Grand National!" Price yelled back, shoveling dust off his shirt and pants with both hands.

"Grand National. The heck. Never heard a that one. Thought that was a horse race over in England!"

"Buick," Price spat out.

"Keeps up pretty good for a city car."

"Yeah. Fastest stock car in America now. Turbo."

"Fastest stock car in America! How 'bout that!" Lowell chuckled and shuffled around to the back gate of the trailer, beginning to untie the maze of frayed rope and wire. He yanked a knot loose with his teeth and held his Bud to the side so it wouldn't get more dust in it.

"You haul those horses kinda fast, don't you, Lowell?" Price said, trying to push himself into the spirit of things.

"Nothin' better for a bronc than a good slam-bang trailer ride. Bounce 'em off the walls a few times, it takes the snot right out of 'em. Makes 'em think twice about crackin' their back with ya."

"Bronc?"

"Oh, yers is broke. Don't you worry about that. We wouldn't mount ya on nothin' with a cold back. We might look a little rough around the edges, but we aim to please. Yers is a pussycat. Guaranteed." Lowell flopped open the rickety gate just as Madilia vaulted out of her stuck door and came around to meet them.

"Told ya about the dust," she said to Price. "You didn't believe me."

"I believe you."

"It'll take the better part of a week to clean all that shit outa yer lungs."

"Yeah, I suppose," he said, raking more dirt out of his hair and trying to get his eyes unglued.

As soon as Lowell pried the gate back, the dun gelding who'd been staring at Price on the road came blasting out backward, then jammed both hocks in the ground and flipped completely over, ramming the saddle horn into his withers. Madilia went right after him like a cattle dog, grabbing the loose reins and jerking his head up. She popped him on the ass with the tip of the rein and the dun leaped to all fours and shook himself, with a dismayed look in his eye. He spun around in a tight circle, farting in short staccato bursts and raising more dust. Madilia kept snapping the rein and spinning around with him in a circle while the oxbow stirrups rattled and caught him behind the cinch. The dun leaped straight up in the air, all four feet off the ground, screaming like he'd been struck by lightning. As soon as he landed, Madilia bent his head back around to his shoulder with the rein, slipped her red boot in the stirrup, and swung a leg up over him. The whole thing happened in a blink, and Price thought he might be falling in love again. "Hard to believe he's got half a dozen rides in him and he's still goosy about the cinch." Lowell chortled as they both watched his daughter reach back with her spurs and dig the horse deep in the flank, then turn his head loose. The dun jumped out at a wide-open, hell-bent-for-leather gallop, then jammed to a stop and began to buck for all he was worth. "See what I mean about these half-breed women, Price? You don't wanna mess with 'em." Lowell laughed and nudged Price's arm with his elbow, then guzzled on his beer as they watched Madilia lay back on the cantle and rake the bronc savagely across the shoulders with both heels. Price just stood there, stupefied. He hadn't seen anything like it since the days of the great Casey Tibbs. "She'll ride just about anything with hair on it," Lowell said, and walked back to the trailer, pulling the two other horses out. He handed one set of reins to Price and nodded toward the blue horizon. "This one here's a veteran. Jest give him his head and point him. He'll do all the rest. Now we best grab leather. We got miles to put on."

They took off at a killing jog, with Madilia finally getting the dun lined out to a broken, humpbacked trot. Whenever the gelding tried to crack his back with her, she'd dig into him with the spurs again and pop him with her heeling rope. After about a mile and a half of this routine he began to drop his head and give in to the bridle, sweat leaching off his back cinch in frothy white ribbons. Price tried to keep pace, stealing glimpses at Madilia and finding his seat in the old broken-down stock saddle. Her father got after the Budweiser right away, thrashing around in his saddlebags and letting the reins flop. He offered a can out to Price, who politely refused. "Suit yerself. I find it helps a man git down on a horse's spine jest a little bit better. Horse seems to sense it when a man's stone sober."

For more than an hour, the three of them never broke out of this jagged, spine-jamming trot. It didn't matter what kind of terrain they covered—sandy creek bottoms, shale slopes, open plains riddled with prairie dog holes—the jog never altered. Price's gelding had a jackhammer stride that rattled every tooth in his head. They crashed through cactus, straight down sheer twelve-foot embankments into thick brush then came out splashing into murky creeks, with unseen boulders and cedar stumps jutting up at them like rusty bayonets. They scrambled up the opposite banks, the ground giving loose in long slabs of crumbling clay; finally gaining footing on the flat tableland above, then weaving through more cactus and sudden holes where whole villages of prairie dogs chirped at them manically as they trespassed in their domain. They jogged on in silence, and the pace never changed. Price felt himself being towed along, not so much by his horse but by Lowell's intent. Price watched him standing long in the stirrups, leaning slightly forward over the horn, hands absolutely still, as he gazed out over his gelding's ears for the herd. It was a gaze that seemed to go back a good two hundred years.

They moved on into higher country and finally reached the top of a long grassy table that offered a clear view in every possible direction. Up till now they hadn't seen a single cow, calf, or yearling, and they must have covered at least eight miles of country. Nothing was out there but the awesome, far-flung prairie, which more and more took on the aspect of some foreign planet. He watched Madilia, sitting calmly now in the saddle, with one leg hooked around the saddle horn. Her eyes were following the same line of vision as her father's, out across the vast, sprawling flatland. Lowell was squinting through a miniature pair of camouflage-green binoculars, the kind you'd buy in an army surplus store, slowly scanning the horizon from left to right. Not a word had passed between the three of them since they'd left the truck and trailer. It was as if the land itself had put them in their rightful place and stripped the need for idle talk. Price watched Madilia's eyes. He went inside them and fell into a stupid spell about her heritage. He was connecting her directly now to Crazy Horse and the Oglala warrior nation. He was losing himself in the saddle. He had to hold on to keep from keeling over suddenly. Maybe it was the dust and the road fatigue. A sharp scream came out of him. He was sure it was him, although the pitch of it and its sudden eruption gave him the sense he was maybe temporarily possessed. It reminded him of the way a burro will cut loose, for no apparent reason, in the dead of night. His borrowed horse bolted, then locked up solid and pinned his dark ears back, waiting for something even more weird to follow. Madilia slowly turned to him and smiled softly, but Lowell never took his eyes away from the pair of binoculars. Maybe he was deaf, Price thought. There was no denying a scream had come from his throat. "I was just trying to see how far my voice would carry out here," he said by way of apology to Madilia, but she just turned her attention back to her father and waited.

"Don't see cow one," Lowell said softly, eyes still glued to the lenses.

"I bet they're over on the other side of Pipestone," his daughter replied.

"I'll bet a man could yell his head off out here and nobody'd ever hear him," Price continued. "A man could die out here yelling his fool head off."

"Some have," Lowell said, as he kept pivoting slowly in the saddle, with both his big meaty hands cradling the glass to his eyes. His elbows were locked solid against his ribs to steady his gaze. "My guess is they're over there on Red Table. See all this land here, Price? All this yer eyeballin' right now fell under what they called the Homestead Act. Probably the very last Sioux land that fell into white men's hands. Happened back when Ulysses S. Grant became President. You remember him? Whupped the stew outa the South. He's the one opened all this back up for white settlement. Had no business doin' it either, tell ya the damn truth. Broke every treaty in the book. Every promise we ever made. But here we are now, and that's the way it happened. I'm a half-breed myself, so I got no call to be passin' judgment on either side of the fence." Lowell's pivoting stopped, and he fixed on a distant spot in the immense landscape. He motioned for Price to pull up next to him while he adjusted the focus on the lenses. "Price, I want you to see somethin' here. Come on up here alongside me." Price nudged his horse up next to Lowell's and took the binoculars, as Lowell placed his massive hand on the back of Price's neck to guide his vision. It made Price feel like he was about nine years old. He was afraid he might cry out again, for no reason, or break down in some terribly injured part of himself that was forever missing a father. "You see that gray knob just below the rim of that table out there? Out past the reef. You know what that is?" Price tried to focus through the tiny eyepieces, but all he saw was a distant wall of rock, fringed with scrub pine. "I'll bet ya dollars to doughnuts there's a buffalo skull buried in that knob. You can tell by the color. See how it's kinda yellowish around the edges? That's the horn bone stickin' out." Price wanted desperately to see this apparition but couldn't nail it down. "We're gonna ride on over there and dig it out. It's on our way anyhow. You can take it back home with ya as a souvenir. Hang it on yer wall and brag on it some, back there in Ioway or wherever it is you come from."

"Kentucky."

"Kentucky, then. They got many buffalo in Kentucky?"

"I believe they used to."

"Then it oughta be a real conversation piece for ya."

They resumed their jog as Lowell returned the binoculars to his saddlebag and fished for another beer. He offered one out to Price again but got the same refusal.

"Whatsa matter? Budweiser's not yer brand?"

"No; I just bloat up on beer."

"Kentucky bourbon must be yer game, huh?"

They descended the steep wall of the high table, down into the grassland floor. Lowell turned himself all the way around in the saddle to speak to Price, mashing his big hand down on the horse's rump. "Me and the daughter have made some strange discoveries out here. Found us an old buffalo robe in a cave once that had three carbines wrapped up in it. All rusted out and the stocks were eaten away by the wind, but they dated back to the 1890s."

"No kidding."

"Found a locket too, with an old faded photograph of a young girl. Couldn't hardly make out the face, but there was a shank of yellow hair in there with it. Hair like silk. Musta been an old hideout. Badlands've always been famous for hiding outlaws and such."

"I suppose so."

"Yer not hidin' out, are ya, Price?" As Lowell asked him this he turned back toward the head of his horse and kept pointing him straight down the slope, sipping on his beer. Price felt a slight electric sting go through him from the question.

"No; why?"

"Don't make a damn bit a difference to me. A man's a man till he proves himself otherwise."

"Why would I be hiding out?"

"Beats the hell outa me. None a my business anyhow. Lotta loose ends, though. You gotta admit."

"How do you mean?"

"Well, like I said, it ain't my business, but you don't seem to know where the hell you come from or where yer goin', do ya, Price?" Lowell spurred his horse into a jump and loped the rest of the way down the sharp incline, beer-laden saddlebags popping up and down with every stride. Price kept picking his way carefully and watched Lowell as he finally hit the basin at a full gallop and kept right on spurring, while balancing his can of beer out to the side.

"Lotta loose ends? What's that supposed to mean?" Price asked himself out loud as he studied the steep footing directly in front of him. Madilia drew up alongside him, laughing and pointing at her father, far below, racing across the yawning basin like something out of a Remington painting.

"He's about one day away from the wild, isn't he! Lookit that! Born a hundred years too late is his problem."

"Guess so."

"That horse workin' out all right for ya?"

"Yeah. He's fine. A little choppy, but that's okay."

"He's not too much for ya, is he?" She laughed.

"No. He's just perfect."

" 'Cause we can swap if you want. This one's all trained now." She grinned at him with all her Lakota teeth flashing.

"No, thanks. This one's fine." They edged their way down, two abreast, for a while, then Madilia turned to him, shifting her weight back in the saddle. "What was that scream you let out back there? That yowl."

"What? Oh. That wasn't a scream exactly."

"What was it, then?"

"I told you–I was just testing my voice a little."

"Testing your voice? Are you a singer or something?"

"No. I mean, I was just curious to see how far it would carry in this distance. This space is pretty amazing."

"Sounded a lot more desperate to me."

"Desperate? Like how do you mean?"

"Terrified."

"Terrified? No. Why would I be terrified? There's nothing around."

"Like this," Madilia said, and then let out an unearthly animal wail that had to have come directly from her ancestors. She jabbed the dun in the flanks and leaped out after her father. It was all Price could do to hold back his old gelding from joining the chase and leaving him dumped on the slope.

When he finally reached the bottom, Madilia and her massive father were nowhere in sight. His horse was twitchy and herd-bound now without the others and kept dancing in little circles with his ears pricked. The floor of the basin was deceptive. From their vantage point, high up on the grassy table, it had appeared to be fairly straightforward country, negotiable by spotting outcroppings or marooned cottonwoods in the distance and then simply tracking them point to point to maintain a true line of direction. Now that he was down in the bottom, though, his whole perspective changed. Dry riverbeds and cedar brakes that had seemed to be nothing more than narrow, twisting fissures from the high ground now turned into miniature Grand Canyons when confronted face-to-face. The walls of these chasms dropped straight down, maybe fifteen, twenty feet in most places, and then repeated themselves on the other side. A horseman had the option of either holding his nose and taking the blind plunge straight off the edge and hoping for the best or laboriously picking his way along the rims until he found a gentler descent. The third choice was to ride all the way around the brakes, zigzagging on the flat grassy ground while trying to maintain a visual objective in the distance that approximated a straight line. The problem for Price was that he had no clue what line to follow. Lowell and his daughter had completely vanished. There wasn't even a trace of dust, and no clear tracks were visible in the long grass. Price chose to hold his nose and take the leap. His old gelding was fearless and well accustomed to this kind of challenge, gathering his hocks up underneath him in short, firm strokes, then pricking his ears toward a landing point and catapulting straight toward the rocky bottom. When he landed, the horse was already in a full trot, legs churning for the opposite bank; then he grabbed hold with his front feet and lurched straight up the side like a bighorn sheep. When they arrived at the top, the horse shook himself all over and resumed his jagged trot as though he'd just gotten shed of a nasty fly.

Now Price was completely lost, and he knew it. He tried to locate the distant knob that Lowell had pointed out to him, but if he hadn't been sure of what he was looking at through the binoculars, now he was dumbfounded. He couldn't even spot the rim with the line of scrub pine. He twisted completely around in the saddle and stared at the overwhelming landscape.

Crows glided out in a lazy line, squawking, then taking nosedives at one another. High above him, a hawk floated with its wings splayed out stiff, like giant arms. Price thought he could see its tiny head across the distance, jerking back and forth in search of some slight movement from earth. He waved his arms at the bird, but his horse got startled by this sudden movement and bolted. Price gathered up the reins and got him back to a nervous walk. He grabbed a shank of the black mane and ran it through his fingers, thinking this might bring him back around to some sense of the present and his lost predicament, but his attention was frazzled and edgy. He was shocked by the sight of his own hands. His knuckles seemed to be standing out, more prominent than usual. The broad fingernail on his index finger seemed even broader and the bulging callus beneath it. His hands became his father's hands, and he had to pry his eyes away, back to the sky, searching for the hanging hawk, but it had vanished. He kept hearing its shrill screech but couldn't spot it. The crows had landed off to his left and were fighting over the carcass of a young jackrabbit, playing tug-of-war with its intestines. He wanted to make sure this was taking place and reined his horse toward the flapping huddle, and when they flew off, cawing, he was satisfied. He stared down at the rabbit's dead head. A blue film cloaked its eyes, but the dark pupils were still staring out. As soon as he walked his horse on, the crows returned and started back up with their squabbling.

The rhythm of his horse's walk seemed to deepen the trance that Price felt himself falling into. He listened to the dull thud of the hooves and the way the sound changed when they entered tall grass. He heard the long tail switch at flies and the occasional snort as the horse cleared dust from his nostrils; the squeak of old leather. The whole presence of the horse startled him. The rolling motion of the shoulders and him up on top, the human passenger. Then he felt himself dissolve. He couldn't tell where the inside of his thighs left off and the saddle fenders began. The pulsing motion of his spine wasn't his own. It belonged to the horse. He was simply dumb cargo.

They creaked along to the brink of another gorge, and this time Price didn't even check the horse. He just grabbed mane and let him drop straight over the side into the unknown. He slacked the reins completely and allowed the bay to wander up the creekbed, slapping through rocks and picking gullies where the rain had cut deep black ruts. He thought if he wandered long enough, he'd get good and lost. He'd get so hopelessly lost that he'd be forced into some part of himself that he'd never known before. Some part he'd be forced to meet up with. The proposition thrilled and terrified him. It was the mind that wouldn't cooperate. He couldn't control the picturings. There was no rhyme or reason to their appearance. He watched them pop up in his head as though he were sitting in a Wednesday matinee from long ago, with no one else in the theater. He saw John Wayne wearing a buffalo coat. President Bush in a baseball cap, with a tie on. Bombs falling on Baghdad. Bombs seen from high above as though he were looking straight down through the hatch. The fat, self-satisfied face of General Schwarzkopf. A boy swinging a sledgehammer at the Berlin Wall and not making a dent. Pictures of news. Pictures of faces making news. Pictures of crows and hawks. A dead rabbit's head. Then Madilia. Her eyes. Her violent, magnificent eyes.

7/91
(Belvidere, South Dakota)

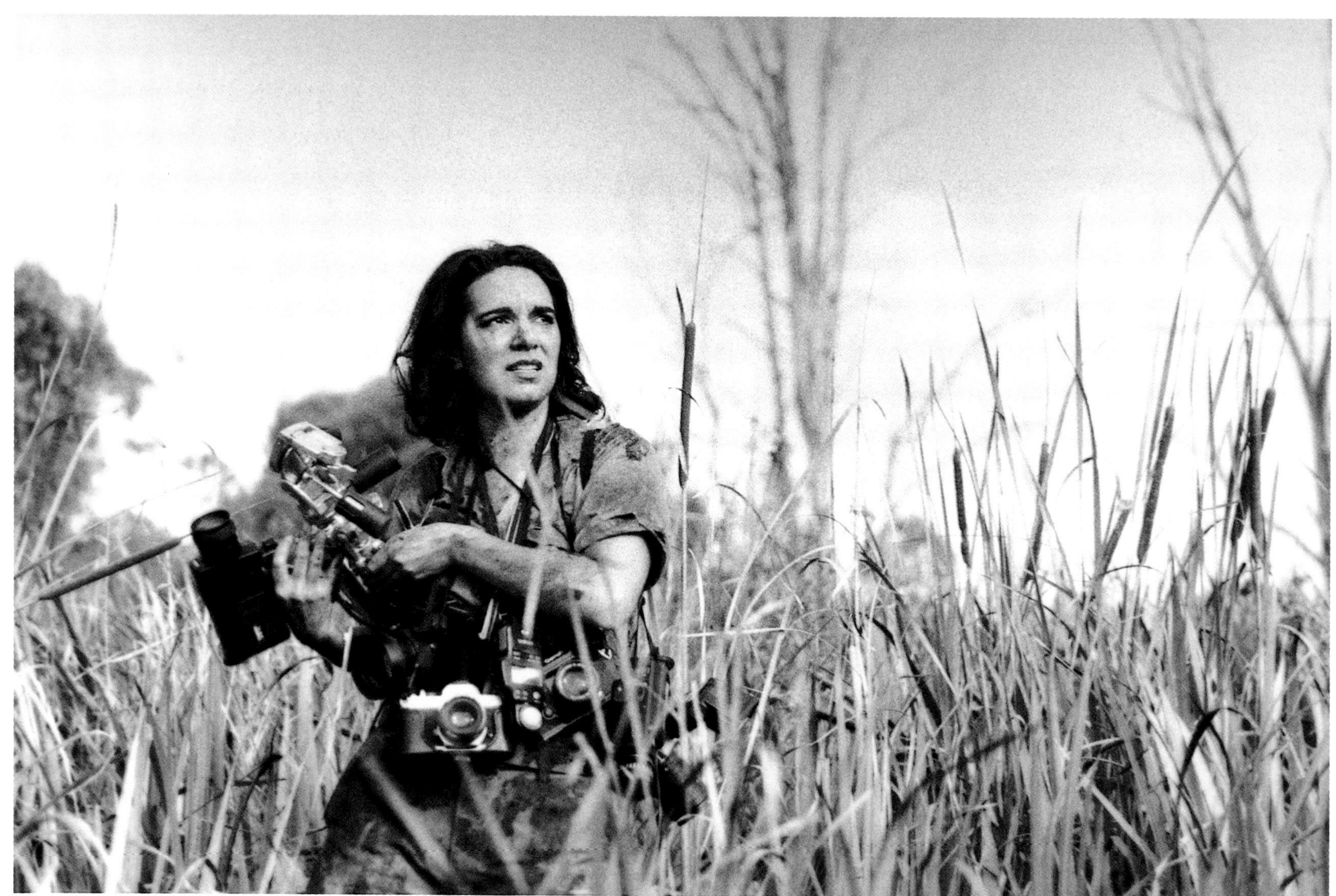

Tracey Moffatt

Selected Biography

1960
Born in Brisbane

1982
Graduates from Queensland College of Art, Brisbane in Visual Communications

1983–
Lives and works in Sydney

Solo Exhibitions

1997
"Tracey Moffatt," Galerie Andreas Weiss, Berlin

"Tracey Moffatt," L.A. Galerie, Frankfurt

1995
"Short Takes," ArtPace, San Antonio

"GUAPA (Good Looking)," Mori Gallery, Sydney

1994
"Scarred for Life," Karyn Lovegrove Gallery, Melbourne

1992
"Pet Thang," Mori Gallery, Sydney

"Tracey Moffatt," Centre for Contemporary Arts, Glasgow

1989
"Something More," Australian Centre for Photography, Sydney

Group Exhibitions

1997
"Group Show," Matthew Marks Gallery, New York
"Truth: Echoes of Art in an Age of Endless Conclusions," Site Santa Fe, Santa Fe, New Mexico
"Future, Present, Past," 47th Venice Biennale, Venice
"Printemps de Cahors," city festival in Cahors, France
"Campo 6: The Spiral Village," Bonnefanten Museum, Maastricht

1996
"Jurassic Technologies Revenant," 10th Biennale of Sydney, Sydney
"The Dematerialization of Art at the End of the Millennium," 23rd Bienal de São Paulo, São Paulo
"Campo 6: The Spiral Village," Galleria Civica, Museo d'Arte Moderne e Contemporanea, Turin

1995

"Antipodean Currents: Ten Contemporary Artists from Australia," Guggenheim Museum Soho, New York

"Jun Nguyen-Hatsushiba, Tracey Moffatt, Joseph Daun," ArtPace, San Antonio

"Australian Perspecta 1995," Art Gallery of New South Wales, Sydney

1994

"Localities of Desire: Contemporary Art in an International World," Museum of Contemporary Art, Sydney

"Reflections of a Nation," National Portrait Gallery, Canberra

"Power Works," Govett-Brewster Art Gallery, New Plymouth, New Zealand

1992

"The Boundary Rider," 9th Biennale of Sydney, Sydney

"Artists' Projects," Adelaide Festival Hall, Adelaide

1991

"From the Empire's End," Circulo de Bellas Artes, Madrid

"Twenty Contemporary Australian Photographers," National Gallery of Victoria, Melbourne, and Art Gallery of New South Wales, Sydney

1990

"Satellite Cultures," The New Museum of Contemporary Art, New York

1988

"Shades of Light," National Gallery of Australia, Canberra

1987

"Art and Aboriginality," Aspex Gallery, Portsmouth, England

1986

"Aboriginal and Islander Photographers," Aboriginal Artists Gallery, Sydney

1984

"Pictures for Cities," Artspace, Sydney

Selected Films and Videos

1997

Heaven, twenty-eight minute video

1993–95

Music videos for INXS, "The Messenger"; Ruby Hunter, "Let My Children Be"; Christine Anu, "My Island Home"

1993

Bedevil, ninety-minute film (Official Selection, Cannes International Film Festival)

1990

Night Cries: A Rural Tragedy, seventeen-minute film (Official Selection, Cannes International Film Festival)

1988

Moodeitj-Yorgas, twenty-two minute documentary video

A Change of Face, three-part, three-hour documentary for SBS-TV

Watch Out, five-minute video

1987

Nice Colored Girls, sixteen-minute film

1985

The Rainbow Serpent, six-part, three-hour documentary for SBS-TV

Selected Bibliography

Jayamanne, Laleen. "'Love Me Tender, Love Me True, Never Let Me Go…': A Sri Lankan Reading of Tracey Moffatt's *Night Cries: A Rural Tragedy.*" In *Feminism and the Politics of Difference*. Ed. Sneja Gunew and Anna Yeatman. St. Leonard, Australia: Allen & Unwin, 1993, pp. 73–84.

Martin, Adrian. "Tracey Moffatt: The Go-Between." *World Art* 2 (1995), pp. 24–29.

Mellencamp, Patricia. "Haunted History: Tracey Moffatt and Julie Dash." *Discourse* 16, no. 2 (Winter 1993/94), p 127–63. Reprinted in Patricia Mellencamp, *A Fine Romance: Five Ages of Film Feminism* (Philadelphia: Temple University Press, 1995, pp. 1–77.

Sirmans, Franklin. "Tracey Moffatt: So Many Stories to Tell." *Flash Art*, no. 195 (Summer 1997), pp. 118–21.

Tracey Moffatt: Fever Pitch. Annandale, Australia: Piper Press, 1995. Essays by Tracey Moffatt and Gael Newton.

Checklist of Works

Night Cries: A Rural Tragedy, 1989
35 mm film shown on video laser disk
17 minutes
Courtesy Women Make Movies, Inc.

GUAPA (Good Looking), 1995
10 black-and-white photographs on chromogenic paper
30 x 39 3/8 inches each

Up in the Sky, 1997
25 offset photographs
28 3/8 x 39 3/4 inches each

Heaven, 1997
videotape
28 minutes

Staff

Director
Michael Govan

Curatorial Assistant
Barbara Clausen

Curator
Lynne Cooke

Assistant Director
Stephen Dewhurst

Security & Visitor Services
Steven Evans

Development and Public Affairs Assistant
Heidi Fichtner

Finance/Graphics
Laura Fields

Development Coordinator
Evonne Gallardo

Editor
Karen J. Kelly

Book Sales Manager
Michelle Marozik

Consulting Director of Poetry Series
Brighde Mullins

Education Coordinator
Scott Myers

Director of Operations
James Schaeufele

Director of Digital Media
Sara Schnittjer Tucker

Executive Assistant
Alan Yamahata

Board of Trustees

Dia Art Council*

Janet and Gilbert de Botton
Frances and John Bowes
Sandra J. Brant
Constance R. Caplan
Jay Chiat
Jan Cowles
Douglas S. Cramer
Frances R. Dittmer
Valerie and John C. Evans
Doris and Don Fisher
Saul A. Fox
Jenny and Alan Gibbs
Milly and
Arne Glimcher
Helyn and
Ralph I. Goldenberg
Ray A. Graham III
Nancy and Steven Grand-Jean
Linda and Anthony Grant
Mimi and Peter Haas
Frederick B. Henry
Jane Hertzmark
Marieluise Hessel
Tom Healy and
Fred Hochberg
Elizabeth and Sidney S. Kahn
Simone and Paulo Klabin
Wanda Mangia Klabin
Werner Kramarsky
Anne and Patrick Lannan
Gretchen and Howard Leach
Ann Tenenbaum and
Thomas H. Lee
John McCaw
Linda and Harry Macklowe
Nancy and Robert Magoon
Maria and Jerry Markowitz
Eileen and Peter Norton
Nancy and Steven H. Oliver
Linda Pace
Ellen and Max Palevsky
Giovanna and
Giuseppe Panza di Biumo
Miuccia Prada and
Patrizio Bertelli
Emily Rauh Pulitzer
Louise and Leonard Riggio
Leanne and
George R. Roberts
Kathy and Keith Sachs
Hannelore and
Rudolph Schulhof
Helen and Charles R. Schwab
Lea H. Simonds
Emily and Jerry Spiegel
Dorie and Paul Sternberg
Norah and Norman Stone
Susy and Jack Wadsworth
Nancy Brown Wellin
Pat and Bill Wilson
Barbara and
Charles B. Wright
Virginia and Bagley Wright

* The Dia Art Council is Dia's major annual support group.